ULTRA MARRIAGE

Going the Distance One Moment at a Time

MIKE BELLINI

Scripture taken from the HOLY BIBLE, NEW INTERNATIONAL VERSION© Copyright©1973, 1978, 1984 by International Bible Society. Use by permission of Zondervan Publishing House All rights reserved. The "NIV" and "New International Version" trademarks are registered in the United States Patent and Trademark Office by International Bible Society. Use of either trademark requires the permission of International Bible Society.

Any internet addresses or links contained in this book are accurate at the time of publication.

Printed in the United States of America

ISBN softcover: 978-1-948693-09-7

ISBN eBook: 978-1-948693-11-0

Library of Congress Registration Number: TXu 2-294-302

Cover design by Tom Prather, The Blue Wave Video Production Agency.

Books may be ordered at: www.TheUltraMarriage.com

Carlisle Printing
OF WALNUT CREEK LTD

Layout & Design | Diana Yoder

800.927.4196 · carlisleprinting.com

2673 Township Road 421 · Sugarcreek, Ohio 44681

Cindy,

You met me right where I was and have continued
to walk with me hand-in-hand along this rocky road
of life. Thank you for your unwavering love, support,
forgiveness, and grace, and for helping me become every
bit of the man I am still becoming.

P.S. Maybe ... just maybe, it was a date after all.

ULTRA MARRIAGE

ACT I: FINDING ME

ACT II, PART 1: BECOMING WE

ACT II, PART 2: PRIORITY

ACT III: HUMILITY

Ultra Marriage is packed with pearls that every single married couple can benefit from. It's an excellent read that touches every emotion while challenging us to grasp that "we are creatures built for relationship, not for things and accomplishments." You will learn through story how to up-level your individual lives by way of up-leveling your marriage. You will laugh, you'll cry, you won't want to put it down. Marriage should not be "an anchor but a sail ... we get married to double our sails and capture more of the tailwind so we can explore and experience more than we can on our own, and become much more in the process." Thank you for showing us that the best self-development begins with our most sacred human relationship, our marriage.

-Amy Tucker, CEO/Creator of Salty Britches

AUTHOR'S NOTE

There are few people from whom I would feel as blessed to receive an endorsement for this book than Amy Tucker. Amy is a wife, mother, and entrepreneur. I first heard Amy on a podcast, passionately telling the story of how she created the product Salty Britches and started her own company from the ground up. She also described the close relationship she has with her husband, and how he encouraged her to go all in when it was becoming clear that she had a special product. She donates a tube to the United States military for every tube sold.

Salty Britches is a saving grace for long-distance runners. Inscribed on every tube is *Philippians 4:13*. That verse of scripture has become known to many as a declaration that we can do anything. What it means in full context, however, is that we can endure all things, the good and the bad, and rejoice through it all, because we are strengthened by something far more powerful than ourselves. Amy has created a product that helps people do just that.

I see marriage in a similar light. Husbands and wives can endure anything life throws at them, the good times and the bad, because they have a combined strength that was created to last. By not only enduring but also rejoicing at every twist and turn with our spouse, we experience an exhilarating adventure unlike any other.

Thank you, Amy, for being such a strong, faithful, loving example for all of us to follow.

INTRODUCTION

"Life is not the amount of breaths you take, it's the moments that take your breath away."

- *Hitch*

The instant I saw her, I knew she was different. Her infectious energy and illuminating smile captured my immediate attention and eventually my heart. Twenty-five years later, nothing has changed.

Well, some things have changed. None of us avoid the fluctuations of life. As for me and my wife, we have remained unwavering and thriving. With each other. Just thinking about her still makes me smile like nothing and no one else can.

We are not special by any means. I grew up an average kid in a small New England town. My wife is from an even smaller town in the farm country of Tennessee. The combined population of our birthplaces could not fill the seats in Fenway Park.

If we are not unique, well-known, or overcomers of an extraordinary hardship, why am I writing this book? The idea came in January 2020 when I was reading another book about marriage. I couldn't relate. My wife and I have had a very different relationship than what was portrayed, so I put it down and wondered, "If I were to write a book about marriage in a way that someone like me could relate to, what would it be like?"

As happens often when a wild idea sprouts, doubt set in. Who am I to write a book? Do I even have a meaningful story to tell? What benefit can I offer from my experience? Why follow through with this crazy notion of writing my own book?

Why? For the very reason that my wife and I are just like most people—but with a marriage that is unlike most. We have faced the common fears and limitations that everyone has and have created a marriage that is uncommon by today's standards. That isn't just my own sentiment. Friends have shared how inspired they are at what they see in our marriage. Some have expressed gratitude for the example we set of what a marriage can be like and that their kids get to see it too. An acquaintance told us how wonderful it was to see us holding hands at a high school football game. Let's face it, we have not done marriage very well in our culture, and it seems to be getting worse. If something as simple as holding hands in public has become out of the ordinary, we need a serious change of heart.

I have recently taken up the sport of competitive running. Truthfully, I have never liked running. "It's painful. How much longer until it's over?" is what I would repeat on a mental recording the entire time I was moving my legs. However, I started running in my 40s for one simple reason, to see how far I can go. To push myself until I reach my limit, then figure out how to go even farther.

Marriage can be like that, but it isn't a sprint or even a marathon. It is a lifelong ultramarathon. The only way to make it to the finish line of an ultra is to focus on one step at a time. If you focus on the entirety of the race at once, it is easy to become overwhelmed and doubt can quickly take over. Whether it is thirty-one, fifty, one hundred, or more miles to the finish, you must focus on simply executing in the present, then continuing to execute one step at a time after.

The difficult reality is that marriage is not easy. It takes effort— and a lot of it. There is no secret recipe that everyone can copy to get the result we all desire. There aren't "Five Steps" to the marriage you want. So how have my wife and I kept our flame burning continuously for over a quarter century? That was the question I asked myself when pondering the concept for a book about marriage. The answer came in a single word: Moments.

Maintaining a long-lasting marital relationship with a love that continuously grows, each present moment must be the focus, and embraced as something special. That doesn't mean all moments are good or pleasurable. Like running a race, the only way to make it to the finish line is to work through the difficulties, learn from the pain, keep going and continue growing every step of the way.

To be clear, this is not a "How To" book. It is more of a "What To" story. I can't tell you how to fix your marriage. I can't force you to give the effort it takes to make it wonderful. However, I *can* tell you what my wife and I have faced and what has led us from that first glimpse of each other to, all these years later, still seeing that same sparkle in each other's eyes, and still striving to run the race with all our gusto. My hope is that you will relate to something, or many things, we have experienced that will help you learn, remember, or restore what can make your current or future marriage greater than you could ever imagine.

When 2019 came to a close, before this book was even a thought, I wrote down four primary pursuits for the upcoming year. One of those read, "Deepen my bond and connection with my wife." Little did I know that remembering and writing about our marriage would help fulfill that promise in a powerful and profound way.

This book is about the moments that have had the greatest impact on our relationship over time. Moments of decision. Moments of distress. Moments of exhilaration. Moments of pain. These are sixteen moments that have shaped what we have, what we have become together, and why we are even more excited about the future, even after twenty-five fantastic years together.

And if two ordinary people like us can build an extraordinary marriage, so can you! God bless you on this amazing and wonderful ultra-journey.

ACT I

FINDING ME

THE SECRET TO LIFE

Curly: Do you know what the secret of life is? One thing. Just one thing.

Mitch: That's great, but what's the one thing?

Curly: That's what you've gotta figure out.

- City Slickers

What is the secret to life? The asking and answering of this very question started a journey that led me out of a life of insecurity and worry and made me the person I am today, primarily through the moments recounted in this book. Changing, growing, and becoming the best version of ourselves takes truthful introspection of what has shaped our worldview. We need to know the answers to questions such as: What do we really think, and why do we think that way? Are those thoughts and beliefs valid, or have they simply become habitual, based on experiences we never consciously chose to have? The first significant moment for my marriage was built upon the need to answer these meaningful questions.

The dominant influences in my life and on my character as a teenager and young adult were television and movies. That's right, afternoon sitcoms and HBO were my primary coaches and teachers in life. Unfortunately, I did not have strong male role models to lead me on a different path at a young age. I was so extremely introverted, shy, and self-conscious, that I hardly talked to girls at all. In fact, I was terrified of them! Whenever I tried, the words came out mostly as a garbled concoction of awkward one-liners. In high school, there may have been three or four girls whom I regularly talked to; and by "regularly," I mean once a week, sitting next to them in class.

By the time I was a senior in college, I was the only 21-year-old male virgin on campus and probably in all of collegiate America. At least, that's what it felt like. Oh, if I could speak to that young, insecure little guy, I would tell him that the most noble, beneficial, and rewarding path to take is to actually embrace virginity until marriage. I know that concept seems antiquated or impossible to some today, and it isn't so relevant for this book, but there are many reasons why I still believe it to be true. Marrying a soul mate opened my eyes to that idea, but I did not understand it back in college.

Foolishly, I jumped at the chance to date the first girl who showed real interest in me, even though we were opposites and mostly incompatible. As you might guess, it was fun for a little while but quickly turned into a disastrous relationship. We were dating for all the wrong reasons and drug it on much longer than we should have. The awkward reality was that I felt a greater sense of self-worth because I had a girlfriend for the first time in my life. I finally felt like a real man. Sadly, I had given the keys of my significance to this girl, and when she wanted to break it off, I snapped. I very nearly had an emotional breakdown, even though I knew it would never have worked between us. I had been alone for twenty-one years, with her for less than one year, and believed I would again be alone, this time for the rest of my life.

The months following the breakup became a time of deep self-reflection. I didn't recognize it then, but it is clear to me now that I was in depression. College had been a safe haven for an introvert like me. Friends were all around. Something was always happening. But now, I found myself with no job, no girlfriend, and no vision for a hopeful future. My prolonged despair concerned my mom and seemed to anger my dad. I alienated my best friend. People treated me differently, as though I were acting strange. I was.

Through the sadness and self-loathing, there was one person who saw past the exterior to who I was at the core and who I was destined to become. One person who didn't treat me any differently because of my outward behavior, but treated me as he had any other time in my life. Only one person who acted as if everything was okay, as if I were okay. This person not only refused to pull away from me like others did, but he also leaned in and got closer. Whether it was intentional or not, he changed the direction of my life and ultimately helped set the foundation of my marriage. Thank God for people like this in our lives, who see past our pain and emotional reactions and lift us up with confidence and unwavering encouragement. We need these people to walk with us through the valleys, keeping their eyes and ours on the peaks. For me, this person was my grandfather.

My grandfather wasn't touchy-feely. He didn't hug, kiss, or say "I love you." He was cynical and guarded, with a sarcastic wit and sly smile that seemed designed to keep others at arm's length. He was chiseled from the greatest generation, having fought in the Philippines in World War II. When I was a kid, I had difficulty seeing through his walled exterior. As I look back, I now recognize the love and care he always had for me. While we were growing up, my sister and I slept over at my grandparents' house most Saturday nights, often playing poker for pennies, and went to church with them on Sundays. My grandfather pitched me whiffle balls in their side yard, and we watched Yankee games together—he was a big fan, so I became a big fan. He took me fishing, showed me how to mount antlers from a deer he hunted, took me for my very first drive when I got my learner's permit, and helped me fix my car when it broke down. He was always there, no matter what. "This kid's going places," he would often tell other people, with a smile and a nod toward me.

We often worked nights together at my father's liquor store. He would bring two desserts, one for each of us, that we'd eat with our coffee after the evening rush, usually with the baseball game on television in the background. After closing, we got in our separate cars, and I followed him along the highway until he took the exit toward his house while I continued on to mine. Before he turned off, I'd drive by and see his left hand lifted by the driver's window, giving me one last wave goodnight.

I don't remember what we talked about on the nights we worked together, except for one conversation. I was in those dark months after college, having reached a precipice of emotion, desperate for direction and some wisdom I could hang my hat on. He was the last person most of our family would consider asking for advice, but not me. Not that night. Perhaps it was because he was the oldest person I knew, had been to war, traveled a little, raised two boys, and recently celebrated his fiftieth wedding anniversary. Maybe it was realizing all the times he was there, or how he treated me with respect and confidence, when others looked at me as if I was a leper. Quite possibly, it was just a voice inside saying, "Ask him … because there is no one else to ask."

I remember exactly where I was standing, in front of the door that opened the walk-in cooler. It was late. There were no customers in the store. What we were actually discussing that led to the question, I have no idea, but I remember actively searching—seeking an answer—needing something to turn my mind and emotions around. Some meaning. Something I could believe in. We stood face to face, man to man, and I looked up at him sincerely, asking with a heavy, vulnerable heart, "What do you think is the secret to life?"

His response was so far from what I expected, it was jarring. Like when you are in the middle of an intense situation, about to freak out, and somebody asks a simple, completely unrelated question like "What's your favorite color?" Suddenly you are snapped out of the intensity for a second, breaking the mental loop you were stuck in.

Without deliberation or hesitation, he replied, "I think you need to find a good woman."

Excuse me? To the most important question I've ever asked anyone, your answer is just some basic, old-fashioned notion? You mean, the most important thing *after* making a lot of money, finding your passion, or doing what you love, right? You have to be kidding. "Finding a good woman" was precisely what I was trying to avoid thinking about. I'd been thinking about it for too long already and was worn out. I wanted to move on. I wanted something else to focus on.

While I stood shell-shocked, dumbfounded that this man

would have that thought about the secret to life, he began to expound.

"You need someone you have a lot in common with, that you enjoy doing things with, especially as you get older together." His eyes gazed upward while he was talking, reflecting, possibly running through the annals of his eighty years on earth, measuring his own life by this standard.

I believe that God speaks to us in different ways, and I have had a few instances in my life when I was certain He was speaking to me. I was not aware of it in that particular moment, listening to my grandfather contemplate the secret to life and floored by his unexpected response, but it had to be God speaking through him. Through this man whom I had never seen kiss or hug his wife of over fifty years and, for the two decades I had known him, slept in a separate twin bed from her. This man, who had never in my hearing uttered the words *I love you* to anyone, but who had lived a lifetime of unconditional love and loyalty to his wife and family. In a moment when I needed wisdom, this man was talking about something I had never heard him discuss before, a profound truth that would alter the course of my life. It was so off-character, it had to be the work of divine inspiration.

Having been influenced primarily by television and movies as a youth, the meaning I had attached to life up to that moment was very different from what I was hearing from my grandfather. I had been measuring life by the amount of money I had, the expensive things I could afford to buy, and the woman, or number of women, I could attract. I had attached most of my self-esteem to the attainment of those things. My grandfather's perspective on the question about the secret to life tore up those distorted visions. It shredded them to pieces!

Until then, no one had told me how important relationships are. Think about it: When we are young, what are we told is important? Getting good grades. Succeeding in sports. Following the rules. Doing chores around the house. Going to college. Getting a good career. Being successful in whatever we do. No one tells us how important relationships are, particularly the relationship we will eventually have with our spouse when or if we get married. We are all desensitized to the notion of dating and building relationships with the opposite sex. Dating is seen as simply a fun, leisure activity. It is still somewhat a badge of honor to be dating someone. I see parents encouraging and even pushing their teenagers to date. Why? Why do we put so much importance on dating and attracting the opposite sex, without any conversation about the importance of building relationships and finding a partner worthy enough for us to give our whole hearts to? It's no wonder marriages so often fail. We fail to express and represent the importance of it to our children.

Would you say the most important decision of our lives is the spouse we choose? We live with this person, procreate, and raise children with this person. We share our lives with this person in ways that we don't with anyone else. Yet, many of us treat this aspect of our lives as if it is happening *to us*, allowing ourselves to be bounced around by our emotions rather than investing the thought, effort, and care we would in any other desire or passion of the heart.

Reflecting on his eighty years, my grandfather understood this. He was passing wisdom from a lifetime of experience, through the good and the bad, to a twenty-three-year-old in search of meaning.

I was waking up to the realization that I hadn't consciously chosen many of my beliefs. Instead, I simply believed what I saw and heard on television or from friends and celebrities. I had allowed my beliefs and values to be chosen for me, and I wanted to start deciding them for myself. This was a major shift. I wanted to start choosing for myself what to believe about life and why.

For too long, my perspective of relationships with women was focused on instant gratification. Outwardly, I wasn't a womanizer by my actions, but—perhaps worse—I was in my thoughts. I wanted to be a ladies' man, but fear and a sense of decency for how we should treat each other and how men should treat women kept me from becoming someone like that. Regardless, I failed to see the long-term significance and importance of relationships.

You might think this is too heavy, deep, and intense for a teenager to think about. Is it any more pressure than asking them to name their chosen career before they graduate from high school? Is it any less important?

You know the definition of insanity—doing the same thing over and over, but expecting a different result. I can be stubborn in my thoughts and actions, messing up repeatedly, and enduring a lot of pain before deciding to change. However, I needed a different result from the pain I was feeling, and this shift in mindset suggested by my grandfather's advice felt like an antidote. Many people date, break up, find someone else to date, and repeat the cycle over and over with different boyfriends or girlfriends. Unfortunately, the high divorce rate tells us that cycle doesn't seem to change with marriage. I know some amazing couples who, both previously divorced, found wedded bliss with each other. In many cases, it seems it takes the first failed marriage to learn how to make the next one work. At twenty-three, I'd made one mistake with a girl, and I refused to make another one.

I never again wanted to feel the way I felt at that time in my life.

So what did that mean? It meant completely reversing the script in my mind, thinking and believing opposite from how I had thought and believed before. I had to change the definition I had learned about what makes a man and reassess how to calculate my own self-worth. I had to be patient. I had to stop looking at every girl as a potential date or mate and start focusing on myself. I had to work on becoming the best version of me and wait for the right girl to come into my life ... no matter how long it took, because it is too important to rush.

Relationships, especially romantic relationships, are important, the most important thing in life for most of us. If we say that and believe it, our actions should reflect it. We should invest in becoming a great man, woman, boyfriend, or girlfriend, in training to become a great husband and wife. It is no different than how we train for a race, class, career, or anything else. If it is ultimately more important than all of those things, it deserves as much or more care.

We all should take marriage more seriously. What do I mean by that? I mean taking it more seriously than we do our paychecks. I mean making it important right in the beginning and increasing that importance as we move forward. Parents should make it a part of raising their children, modeling it for them and sharing its significance. We should have a clear vision of what we want and take intentional and consistent actions that move us toward it. Taking marriage seriously means doing some of the things I write about in this book, giving it the priority it deserves to thrive and survive.

We pursue things like money, education, business, and personal achievement with reckless abandon, thinking they will fulfill us. We are creatures built for relationships, not for things and accomplishments. We have gotten that twisted. It is time to unwind our thinking.

This moment, when my grandfather hit me with his version of the secret to life, redirected my focus. It eventually led me to becoming the type of man that could attract a soul mate. It led me to the woman I married, and has taken us through twenty-five years together, and counting. It led me to writing this book, to remembering the most significant moments and decisions that have blessed us, and to sharing those moments with you.

IT'S NOT A DATE

Stan: Miss Rhode Island, please describe your idea of a perfect date.

Cheryl: I'd have to say April 25th, because it's not too hot, not too cold, all you need is a light jacket.

- Miss Congeniality

"No, Dad! I have to start taking responsibility for my own mistakes!" It just came out. I'd had enough. Disappointed in myself. Angry for the foolishness. Frustrated at being treated too softly. It all had to stop.

I had just killed my car. A car my father had bought when I entered college. It was only five years old.

"Well," he said, "it'll be all right. We'll get you another car."

That's when I hit a threshold. The kid gloves needed to come off. In a flash of clarity beyond my own experiential wisdom, I rebuked my father's attempt to console by emphatically proclaiming that "I have to start taking responsibility for my own mistakes!" God must have whispered it in my ear—or shouted it at me, then through me.

My father is a good, hard-working man, who has done a lot

for his family. There always seemed to be someone he was taking care of, whether it was my sister and me when we were young, his parents when they got older, or my mother when she had cancer. Unfortunately, that generous side of him was sometimes easy to manipulate, and I took full advantage when I could.

I had finally reached a boiling point with my own behavior. I was tired of making excuses for my mistakes. It wasn't just about the mistakes, either. I had never truly discovered who I was. I had plans to change that, plans to find the real me for the first time in my life. I believed he was somewhere in Georgia. At least, that's where I was going to look for him. Only, I had just destroyed my means of getting there, threatening the adventure I needed more than anything.

After an emotional week of ups and downs, I borrowed my mother's car, withdrew all two thousand dollars from my bank account, packed most of my belongings, and drove south with a friend who was equally dissatisfied with life after college. There was no better time in our lives for a wide-open adventure.

Thinking we had nothing to lose, we committed to living in Atlanta for one year. We would look for jobs and work on personal growth. If we didn't like how things were going after the year, we would simply move back home to New England. We'd either find our destiny or start over.

We rented an inexpensive, roach-infested apartment along a main suburban strip. We bought cheap tennis rackets as a primary form of entertainment and exercise and spent a little time at a sports bar down the street. After three months, I found my dream job at a private investment firm, and my friend was raking in money by working fourteen-hour days at a bank. Things were really looking up, until halfway through our one-year commitment, he moved back to Boston to marry his girlfriend. So much for following through on a pledge!

Of course, the road of destiny comes with surprises and fellow sojourners. Right after my migrant buddy informed me he was leaving, another friend from college called out of the blue. "I hear you're looking for a roommate," he said. "I could use a change myself." Just like that, he moved down to Atlanta, in search of the same inner awareness, and we moved into an apartment together.

For the first time in my life, I was blazing my own trail and finding myself—my passions, beliefs, wants, and values. It can be scary to be yourself and put yourself out there because, if people reject you, they reject you for exactly who you are.

Thankfully, I was stepping into my true self and everything was working out as if it were planned in advance. The tennis racket I'd bought a few months earlier for some cheap recreation served up winds of change that have yet to cease blowing. The apartment complex I moved into with my new roommate offered free tennis lessons every Tuesday night, and a neighbor invited me to go. While we waited our turn just outside the chain linked fence, a female duo was working with the instructor on the court. That is when I saw her for the first time.

She had a joyful exuberance. Mesmerized by her smile and energy, I couldn't take my eyes off her. In the past, I would have immediately started panicking, thinking about what I needed to do to attract her, and hoping she would like me. The new me didn't much care about myself, how I was feeling, and what I might want. I suppressed the attraction, to avoid any unwanted pressure. In a way, I was "fasting" from the thought and pursuit of dating or romantic relationships. It's not that I didn't want to, but I told myself I "couldn't." I had absolved myself, in the name of the Father, Son, and Holy Spirit, from any burden that comes with being attracted to the opposite sex. Amen!

While it is fun to remember and even joke about now, this was a very important step in our pending relationship. If you haven't guessed, I eventually married this girl. When we first met on that tennis court, we were both primarily focused on self-discovery and personal growth. We weren't trying to be anyone else. We weren't trying to do things to manipulate the other to like us. We were stepping into our true nature, our genuine selves, like it or not, take it or leave it. We recognized each other for exactly who we were—the beauty and the imperfections. It was a complete acceptance: first, accepting our own selves for who we were and who we were becoming, and second, accepting each other for exactly the same reasons.

That night, after the first lesson, my neighbor and I, and she and her neighbor, started talking. We sat at a table by the courts for a while getting to know each other. She was wearing a fraternity sweatshirt, the same fraternity to which I belonged in college.

"Is that your boyfriend's?" I slyly asked.

"I don't have a boyfriend," she responded.

Yes! I mean, "Oh." Okay, so I didn't completely suppress the attraction.

A few weeks later, we added two more people to our group and became our own version of the 90s sitcom *Friends*—three guys and three girls who hung out and did life together. We were helping each other through the awkward and often uncomfortable post-college phase with support, fun, and sometimes thought-provoking and deep discussions.

Then came a particular weekend when everyone but me and

my future wife went out of town, the first weekend our group was not getting together since we had formed. So it was just me and her … and it turned into our first official date. That is, if you ask my wife, it was our first date. I contend that it was most definitely *not* a date because, well, I wasn't dating. I was still fasting from it. Perhaps she thought I was just dieting from it and could allow for a little taste. Either way, there was absolutely no intention on my part to do anything remotely related to what someone might consider a dating action. What did we do? Laundry. No one does laundry together and calls it a date, so, clearly, it was not, and was never intended to be, a date!

When we realized that all our other friends were leaving for the weekend, there was an initial awkwardness in the air. Should we do something together? Should we just wait for our friends to get back? I don't recall who spoke first, but we had a clumsy exchange that went something like this:

"Looks like everyone is going away this weekend."

"I'll be here."

"Oh, me too."

"Are you doing anything?"

"I was just going to do laundry and relax."

"Huh. Me too."

"You want to get together and, maybe, watch a movie while we wait for our clothes?"

"Me too … I mean, sure."

So what would become known as the infamous "laundry date" was set. Friday night, two friends getting together to drop off their dirty threads at the community laundry room and then heading to my apartment to watch a movie. No different than a couple of buddies drinking beer and watching a game. Not a date.

Truth be told, I did have a specific objective for the night other than getting my clothes clean. Whatever movie we watched, I wanted her to enjoy it. I thought through all the movies I'd seen recently and picked one that I figured was a shoo-in.

There was one big problem, though. The night before, I'd hardly slept a wink. It was one of those nights when you have difficulty falling asleep, feel like you never slept more than five minutes at a time, and woke up exhausted. The kind of exhausted that makes your head and stomach hurt because your body just wants to shut down and rest. That's how I felt Friday, all day and into the evening. How in the world was I going to stay awake while we watched a movie together? Some of the old thoughts crept in, wondering how it would look when I fell asleep during the movie, alone with her in my apartment, probably snoring and drooling. Thankfully, the pressure was considerably less than it would have felt like in high school or college, because I was not interested in dating, and this was unquestionably just a mutually agreed upon friendship activity.

The night began and ended as expected—sort of. We did our laundry, watched a movie (sitting on separate couches), and, miraculously, I managed to stay awake through it all, late into the night. When the movie ended, we drove back to the laundry room to pick up the rest of our clothes. As we put our baskets in our cars, I closed the back door of my four-door sedan, spun around to say "Goodnight," and her car was already gone! She zipped out of the parking lot. No "goodbye," "goodnight," "thanks," or "see ya later." It was a Christian Bale, Batman-like exit. Poof! There one second, gone the next.

What I didn't find out until years later is that she thought the night actually *was* a date. She sped out of the parking lot, disappointed at my lack of awareness and interest in her. It could not have been a worse ending to a non-date date.

That night could have been a major turning point in our relationship, and I believe it was for all the right reasons. Having solidified that we were not going to consider dating (at least for the immediate future), we set out on a journey over the next couple months of simply being friends and getting to know each other intimately, without the expectation of goals, desires, and the emotional or physical aspect of a "relationship." We were simply drawn to each other and honored that allure by being there for each other. We were building a strong friendship. We talked about hopes, struggles, and beliefs. We talked about family. We talked about school, since she was a first-year teacher and experiencing the insecurities and difficulties of leading a classroom by herself. We talked a lot, about all kinds of things.

After one of the nights our gang of six had gathered at her apartment, everyone left but me. We were talking, and I made a very simple but honest comment.

"You changed your hair," I said.

Honestly, I wasn't trying to win points, impress, or make her feel good. It was just a genuine observation. Sure, her hair looked good—she always looked good—but that wasn't why I made the comment.

I'll never forget the look on her face after I said it. She smiled with a joy that spoke volumes. *He noticed!* It was a genuine comment and an equally genuine response. Me being me, and her being her.

We were becoming authentic versions of ourselves, liking both the person we saw in the mirror and who we saw in each other. That made the attraction between us real and unwavering. Often we pretend to be something or someone we are not in order to attract another person. Pretending gets emotionally exhausting. Being real is easier, but scarier.

It hurts more to know that someone dislikes you for who you truly are, so pretending to be something you aren't seemingly shields you from direct judgment and pain. We often hesitate and fail to take action because we fear the consequences, embarrassment, or potential backlash. When we are young, much of that is influenced by our family structure and environment.

At some point, however, we have to decide for ourselves who we are going to be. If we can get over that initial fear of being rejected, and be who we truly are inside, everything else becomes simpler.

Consider what it takes for professional actors to play a role. They have to think like the character would think, memorize lines, and act in ways the character would act. It's not easy. The best actors in the world get paid tens of millions of dollars to do it for one movie. However, that's what we tend to do every single day. We act based on what we think others expect of us, or in such a way that we believe will make others like us. We act, instead of being. We are human *beings*. We should *be* ourselves rather than *act* like someone we think we *should* be. If a relationship is to last, especially a relationship meant for everlasting love, we must truly be ourselves rather than acting like some other imagined person.

In the months following my move from New England to the Southeast, I spent a lot of time studying how I had acted in my one previous relationship, reflecting on what I did and didn't do well. It was an intensive, postmortem deep dive. What did I say or do that wasn't genuine, but instead was either what I thought she wanted or was something I saw or heard other guys do? What did those words and actions lead to? Did they strengthen the relationship or weaken it? Were those words and actions fair to her, did they respect her, or were they hurtful? What did I do that was selfish, with no regard for her wants or feelings? Did I do or say anything that was completely unselfish? How did those various actions impact the relationship?

I thought back to many comments and interactions in our time together that led to happiness, joy, discourse, tension, and pain for either or both of us. I wanted to learn from the successes and mistakes, in hopes of doing it much better the next time. In a sense, I was building a foundation within myself that would lay the groundwork for a relationship with the tennis-playing, laundry-washing, southern girl who had captivated my heart.

Ironically, or perhaps not, she was also in a prolonged post-relationship period of self-reflection. From what I learned, her previous relationship seemed to have begun like a fairy tale. They had met on vacation in Europe, brought together halfway across the world, enchanted with romance and fate. Destined to live happily ever after. (Blech!) Lucky for me, it was a distanced relationship. In her last year of graduate school at the University of Tennessee, he was working in South Carolina and encouraged her to apply for jobs wherever she wanted, without limiting herself to looking in South Carolina just to be with him. She took that as a sign that he wasn't certain about a long-term commitment, and, like the action-taker she is, she broke it off.

Their Cinderella story was over, at least for the time being. She then set off on the very same quest that I had—to find herself and discover her own heart's desires before electing to give her heart to someone else. It was one of the longest periods in her life that she'd been without a steady boyfriend. She was just that desirable—beautiful, vivacious, and yes, challenging. I can only think of one reason why a man hadn't pledged his eternal love to her yet: because she hadn't fully realized her true self, who she was inside and out as a unique individual, until she gave herself the time to do so. When she finally did, her radiating light was on full display for all to see.

A couple months after our "laundry date," I woke up on her couch after a late-night get-together at her apartment. She was stirring in her bedroom and stepped out just as I was getting up. Something was different. Nothing had happened between us physically, but for the first time, we both admitted that something was happening emotionally. We decided that morning to accept the passion that was budding and building between us and to start dating romantically.

I do wonder what might have been different had I treated our laundry night as an actual date. How would our relationship have progressed if I had tried to romance her or if we had kissed? Would we have skipped over some important time of introspection for us both? Would we have rushed into a romantic relationship and missed getting to know each other's hearts? Would we have put too much pressure on ourselves to "make it work"?

We are overly stimulated by what is around us and too often fail to take time with the most important person we could ever get to know—ourselves. Before we can ever attempt to know someone else, we must first know who *we* are. Understanding someone else's plight is only possible if we truly understand our own.

Lasting relationships don't just happen, they are built. They take intentionality, right from the beginning. And the best, most solid foundation, is to start by finding yourself first. "Know thyself" intimately before giving yourself to another. Then, and only then, can another know and love you for who you really are.

My wife and I found ourselves and built the core of our relationship before we found our future together. It was a process that set a foundation that has been unwavering and unshakable for two and a half decades and counting.

THE EX MARKS THE SPOT

"If we were meant to be together, we would be together."

- *The Vow*

Have you ever recognized a potentially life-altering moment as it was happening in real time? The third significant moment that helped set the foundation for the marriage my wife and I would have was one of those. It was as if I stepped outside of my body and watched it unfold like it was a scene in a movie. In this scene, the lead character was tested with a defining challenge. Only, the lead character was me, the scene was really happening, and how I responded to the circumstance at hand would define the rest of the story.

Things had been going so well in our relationship. We had been dating for several weeks, growing closer, having fun, and discovering more about ourselves and each other. It was a perfect start to an uncomplicated, unplanned, meaningful relationship. Until one night after work when we got together, and she told me the news. This was the kind of news no one wants to hear when they are in a committed relationship.

She looked at me with a sullen expression and proceeded to tell me her ex-boyfriend was coming into town for the weekend and wanted to have lunch.

"What do you think?" she asked hesitantly.

Let's see. I think, *Ahhhhhhhhhhhh!!*

I'm thinking what seemed to be the perfect relationship just got blown up into a mushroom cloud of smoke. I'm thinking I'm in shock, shattered, and enraged. I'm thinking I'm going to be the last single man left in a post-apocalyptic world, like Will Smith in *I Am Legend*, only without the Legend label.

Suddenly, an enormous weight pressed down upon me. This had to be a test, right? Just a hypothetical? It wasn't really happening, was it? I didn't know who this guy was, but let's face it, my relationship with this girl was no comparison to what they shared. In my mind, their connection could be described as destiny, a force of nature, or meant-to-be. They were two young college kids from America who met in Europe, in a bastion of romance, surrounded by the age-old beauty of art and architecture, sipping wine and sampling cheese, as if the universe had planned their chance encounter from the beginning of time. Maybe he was arriving now with a glass slipper to complete the fairy tale.

Conversely, she and I had no such storybook beginning. We met on a tennis court in Georgia's sweltering summer heat. We lived in small apartments. We had no money—at least, I didn't. There were no backdrops of the Eiffel Tower, Swiss Alps, or Venetian gondolas in our pictures. We watched television with our group of friends on Thursday nights, and we once did laundry together. Ho hum.

Making matters worse, my one previous relationship back in

college had stoked a burning fire of jealousy within. That girl had a naturally flirtatious personality that kept me in a constant state of paranoia. In retrospect, I had wanted her to be less of who she truly was, just so I could feel better about myself. That was wrong of me. Instead, I should have risen to become more of my true self—more confident, accepting, and authentic.

Looking forward, I did not want my own potential jealousy or insecurity to weaken another relationship. Not this one. Not with the spitfire I had met on the tennis court, who was just invited to lunch with her former Prince Charming.

Gripped by intense fear and trepidation, I envisioned our relationship being played out in a few directions, and all but one of them ended in heartbreak for me. I could see her returning to him to complete the fairy tale. I could also imagine her becoming conflicted between two men. Perhaps most vividly, I then saw me convincing her not to have lunch with him, and her subsequently resenting me for it.

The only scenario I saw that ended well was to put up no fight whatsoever and completely surrender to her choices about going to the lunch and about him and me. That was the only way to get to the truth, for all of us. After going through one prior relationship being someone I didn't want to be and trying to convince a girl to become something she was not, seeking the ultimate truth was the only desirable option—even if it meant risking the loss of a girl with whom I was falling in love.

The moment felt like hours but was just a few seconds. What happened next can only be explained as another instance of being guided by a Higher Power. I could have replied in any of a dozen ways. I could have been forcefully defensive. I could have been horrendously emotional.

I could have lashed out in panic and ruined our relationship right then and there. I could have easily delayed a response with the excuse that I needed to "think about it." This moment was not only complicated, but also defining. I thought about the kind of person I wanted to be and knew the reaction I needed to give in just a few seconds would be a huge step—either toward or away from that person.

Somehow wisdom prevailed because of another thought that flashed in front of me with immediate conviction. A voice of truth in my head that said, "She will never truly be yours if you aren't willing to risk letting her go."

What did it mean, exactly? It meant that if I convinced her not to go, without her making the decision on her own, there might always be a part of her that wondered, a piece of her that belonged to someone or something else. It was her choice to make, not one I should try to stop her from making. She could never fully be all-in with me unless she decided to cash in her chips from the past, and that is precisely what I wanted. No longer willing to settle for a semblance of a relationship, I wanted all of her. All of us. Or nothing. If there was going to be an "us," we had to let go of anything in the past that could keep us from moving forward. In hopes that we could release the anchor and sail forward unbound and completely free, I had to risk the real chance that she might choose to go back.

All this raced through my mind in a matter of seconds. Without hesitation, I effectively suppressed the person I used to be—fearful, jealous, self-conscious—and became the person I was created to be. I displayed calm and understanding, simply expressing that it was her choice. If she wanted to go, then she should go. My feelings and opinions didn't matter. I was okay with whatever she thought was best.

Ironically, she acted more cautious and uptight about it than I did. It was as if she hoped I would tell her it was a bad idea, to let her off the hook and give her an excuse to avoid confronting the uncomfortable past. A way out was not what she needed, though.

"Lunch day" came quickly. With torturous anticipation, I awoke that morning knowing there was a chance the next time I saw her, post-lunch, could be the last time. I did everything I could to distract myself from thinking about it. It was almost like waiting for the release of your grades in school or the posting of athletes that made the team after tryouts. You know they are coming, you know approximately but not exactly when, and you know they will be final. Pass or fail. Made the team or didn't. No other opportunities, and no more time.

I remember exactly where I was when I eventually saw her that afternoon. I was sitting on the floor of my bedroom, throwing a rubber ball against the wall, playing with my cat, trying to stay distracted. I looked up and saw her in the doorway.

She walked into the room, as light as an angel, and sat down on the floor next to me. Without even a touch, it felt like an embrace. It was a good sign that she was there so soon after the lunch, right? Maybe? What was she about to say?

It took only a minute for her to explain. Admittedly, she had gone to the restaurant unsure and conflicted, but curious if she would feel the way she used to feel about him. She arrived at the restaurant first, was seated at a table, and waited. Then waited a little longer. Finally he arrived. Late. The moment she saw him walk in, she told me as we sat together on the floor, "I knew I was in the wrong place."

The rest of the lunch was a formality. She sat through the

meal only to be courteous, but she never would have known that this chapter had already concluded had she not been courageous enough to go back and read it again. She was free to start or continue writing an entirely new story.

Perhaps my reaction to first hearing about the proposed lunch was like giving her a pen, without knowing if she was going to continue writing the previous chapter or conclude it. Thankfully, she decided to write "The End."

It wasn't until later in our relationship that she admitted my reaction to hearing about the lunch with her ex stunned her. She would have completely understood if I had gotten upset or tried with all my might to convince her not to go. In fact, I think she expected it. It is certainly what I would have expected of myself. With the guidance of Wisdom that I didn't possess on my own, the moment had not played out that way, and our relationship, at least for the foreseeable future, had been sealed.

Success in anything is often dependent on one's willingness to risk losing everything in order to gain everything. That risk is the monster that lurks under the bed in the dark of night. We can't see it, but we envision what it looks like and what it can do to us. It often holds us back, keeping us from pursuing dreams and aspirations that require full surrender and commitment to the process, no matter how long it takes. However, if we can rally the courage and persevere with strength and faith, on the other side of facing the monster are rewards far greater than we can imagine. All of this is just as true in relationships as in any area of our lives.

Put another way, in Matthew 16:25, Jesus told his disciples, "Whoever wants to save their life will lose it, but whoever loses their life for me will find it." If I had succumbed to the fear of losing my relationship with this girl and acted solely to save it,

I would have been playing defense, putting up every formidable barrier possible to keep her from going to lunch with her ex-boyfriend (the monster that threatened to take her away from me). That type of jealous behavior, in what would look like an attempt to protect what we had, might cause us to lose it, whether in that moment or sometime later in life. Jealousy and acting out of fear is a destructive force in any relationship.

Conversely, if I were willing to lose our relationship, to give it up for the greater good, surrendering the outcome to whatever was best for everyone in the long run, eventually I would find what I was meant for, and what we were meant for. Surrendering the fear will eventually lead to finding a life that is far greater than we could ever imagine. That is what I wanted with this girl, and nothing less. It is also what she deserved.

The impact of this moment, of surrendering emotions and personal desires in search of a greater relationship, has extended far beyond just her having lunch with an ex-boyfriend. It spans the entirety of our life together. It takes two people to build a lasting relationship, and there are definitely inherent risks that come with it. We can convince ourselves that we are able to control certain actions or traits of a significant other, but we can't and should never try. In the same way, we can't force someone else to like us, want us, or love us. We have to be willing to let each other go and grow, and become who we both were created to be.

When both people in a relationship refuse to settle for anything less or different than their truest selves, and when there's a spark that turns into a flame that eventually engulfs both in a blissful existence that passes all understanding ... that's when you know you have something that is more than special. You have something that is meant to be.

God put the best things in life on the other side of fear. I am forever indebted to that soft, gentle, wisest of voices that guided us to and through this decisive moment in our lives. It got us to the other side, where everything we wanted and needed was waiting.

MOMENT #4

WHAT IT FEELS LIKE

Skylar: I want you to come to California with me.

Will: You sure about that? How do you know?

Skylar: I don't know. I just know.

- *Good Will Hunting*

"How do you know?" my teenage son asked. "How do you know who the right girl is?"

Whew, an age-old question that may never be answered definitively. I was not at all prepared with an answer for my firstborn. Is it a question that can be measured or solved? I don't know. I mean, I knew when I knew, but I did not know how to explain to my son how he will be able to know. You know?

I don't think there is a one-size-fits-all prescription that can tell us when we know, how we know, and if we know we are with the right match or life partner. I can, however, tell you my experience, because there was a definitive moment my wife and I both knew, without needing to ask and answer any question at all. If you are single, perhaps this can give you an idea of what it might feel like. If you are married, use this as a comparison to your own story, and as an opportunity to reflect and recall what the experience was like. And if you are a parent, this may prepare you to answer the question someday for your kids. Remember what you felt, thought, and believed that catapulted you into your current union.

About a month after enduring the lunch with her ex, my wife (then girlfriend) and I shared our first Valentine's Day together. Standing in the kitchen of her apartment, she cautiously expressed the most powerful three-word phrase in the English language. "I love you," she said, for the first time.

Of course, I reciprocated, but I had already said it once before. Several weeks earlier, I cried out to her—literally—in a drunken stupor. It was not my proudest moment. I took a pass on actually meaning what I had said because of being under the influence of something other than love. This time, on Valentine's Day, it was all true. No outside manipulations. We meant it.

Since our relationship was progressing, we took a road trip to Tampa, Florida, where she met a few of my family members. The first stop was at a restaurant to have lunch with Jiddo, which means "grandpa" in Arabic. He was my grandfather from my mother's side of the family. His parents had emigrated from Lebanon. He was a short, handsome widower, shrewd as a snake, with a sharp wit and childlike curiosity. He owned a restaurant when I was growing up and used to take me behind the bar to help out. He was also a storyteller. Dinner table discussions were rarely boring when he talked about the "old days."

Jiddo was a hard worker. In the mornings, he traveled through town to pick up fresh fish for the restaurant and then tended the bar until closing after midnight. It was a forty-five-minute drive back home, where my grandmother would be waiting up with a hot meal. After they sold the restaurant, my grandmother's health deteriorated, and their roles reversed. She could no longer cook, clean, or do laundry. Jiddo, an old-fashioned hunter-gatherer, took over all household responsibilities. For probably the first time in his life, he learned how to wash clothes. He experimented in the kitchen, sometimes bringing pies over to our house for dessert. Essentially, he traded in his traditional role as provider and protector of his family to become a modern-day homemaker.

None of us realized until after my grandmother passed just how much they loved each other. Seeing Jiddo, who had been a bedrock in his family for decades, fall apart emotionally without the love of his life, the woman he had been with since they were in their mid-teens, brought to light their connection and devotion to one another. It ran deep. It was a steadfast commitment to loving each other. All of a sudden, our eyes were opened to the relationship they had shared—how much they held hands, smooched, picked at each other playfully, cared and sacrificed for each other, and smiled and laughed together—right up until the very end.

He lived with us for a few weeks after her passing, just so he wouldn't be by himself. He would lie on the guest bed, sobbing, feeling lonely. "I never understood why people could think of killing themselves," he once said. "But now I do." It was heart-wrenching to see him that way. That kind of love became a model for what I wanted my own marriage to be like someday.

I was named after Jiddo, though not intentionally. When I was a newborn in the hospital, awaiting surgery to repair a hole in my esophagus, I did not have a name. It was before ultrasounds could definitively tell the sex of a baby in the womb, but my parents had been convinced that I was going to be a girl. So they had a girl's name picked out and hadn't even considered names for a boy. Two days after entering the world, I was still nameless. My parents have not been known to make quick, decisive choices under pressure but were convinced to select a name before the surgery, so they hastily decided to copy both of my grandfathers' names. My dad was named after his father, Peter, but didn't want to have a Junior in our family, so I became Michael Peter, after Jiddo and Grandpa.

There we sat, my girlfriend and I having lunch with my namesake in a local Tampa restaurant. In his late seventies, Jiddo was still a charmer and handsome as ever. I remember the mood of that lunch clearly. It was nice … joyful … peaceful … comforting. It was without expectation or trepidation. It just fit.

I don't recall much of anything else we did on that trip. I just remember that lunch and the drive home after the vacation was over. It was a ride that altered the trajectory of our lives. We had been driving for a few hours, and were traveling north on I-75 just below Atlanta. We were engaged in a conversation that led to some comments about our relationship. A conclusive realization washed over me, over us. One of us, I'm not sure which, uttered a short phrase, a truth that was as real as the southern summer heat.

"I guess this is it," one of us said.

"I guess so," the other agreed. "I guess this is what it feels like."

Until then, we hadn't discussed it at all. I mean, not the slightest mention. It wasn't even a thought. We hadn't wrestled with any of the typical questions that couples tend to consider. It came out of nowhere. Suddenly, at precisely the same moment, we both were struck with the same conviction of where we were in our relationship and where we were going. It really didn't even feel like a choice. It just was. It was us, and would always be us, for the rest of our lives.

You know the inquisitive look on someone's face when they just say "Huh" and look up with their eyebrows raised or the corners of their mouth drooped, having realized something obvious but profound? That's what this moment was like. It was a "Huh" experience. No fireworks, intense emotion, laughing, crying, or shouting for joy. Just, "Huh! I guess this is what it feels like."

That is what it was like to know we were each with the person with whom we would spend the rest of our lives. We didn't have to run down any checklists to make sure each of us embodied the characteristics that the other preferred in a life partner. We didn't have to take a test to see if we were compatible. We didn't have to ask anybody else's opinion. We didn't even have to ask or discuss it with each other. We just knew. It wasn't an option to *not* be together. As sure as the sun comes up in the morning and the stars can be seen on a clear, dark night, we were going to get married.

What was your moment like (if you've had one)? Do some couples really ask questions like: Do I want to marry this person? Can I see myself with this person for the rest of my life? Does he or she have the qualities I want in a spouse? How many couples discuss questions such as: What do you think about our future, or do you see this going anywhere? How many proposals are made with the answer in doubt?

If questions like this are deemed necessary to ask before taking the biggest, most impactful step in life, I have to wonder how solid the relationship's foundation is. If these questions are in our minds at all, are they telltale signs that we might be forcing something that shouldn't be forced? In my opinion, there should be no questions needed, no assessments of the other person or the relationship itself. If these questions exist, do they ever go away, or will they continue throughout the marriage?

Trying to find enough reasons to marry someone is not a basis for marrying them. If anything, the only question might be, "How can I possibly live without this person?"

A couple months later, I began to understand why we were right for each other and why we wanted and needed to be together every day forward under the sun.

We were at an awards banquet for county educators, following my wife's first full year of teaching. The banquet was to honor everyone in education and to recognize exemplary effort and accomplishments. I was her date, and when they announced her name as the recipient of the New Teacher of the Year Award, I felt something inside that I couldn't recall ever feeling as strongly before. I was genuinely happy, excited, and proud for her, to the point of tears.

The emotion grabbed me by complete surprise. I took a second to acknowledge the magnitude of it all and of what it meant. As she walked up to claim her award, my eyes dropped down to the table, gazing at the plates, the glasses, the silverware, the napkins, meditating on what I was feeling. I had never felt that way about *myself* before, and here I was getting choked up over someone else's accolade. It was a small insight into a question that never needed be asked. I cared more for her than I did for myself. Huh, I guess that's what it feels like.

In that car ride home from Tampa, the moment we both knew we were heading toward nuptials, I don't think the words "marriage" or "married" were even spoken. We just knew that what we had is what we would always have, and what we would always want, each and every day, one day at time, until time stops.

Marriage is like an entrance into a new world, a different realm in the journey of life. By the time my wife and I had the epiphany that we were on our way to getting married, we had already crossed the threshold into that new world in our minds, without even realizing it. I think that if you have to decide whether or not you *want* to take that step and *want* to cross that threshold into the new world of marriage, you may not yet be where you need to be in the relationship. For us, it wasn't a question of whether or not we wanted to get married, or even if we wanted to spend the rest of our lives together. We *knew*, for all the right reasons. We had broken free from things that held us back in the past, had become our truest selves, had accepted, liked, and loved each other for exactly who we were.

As I'm writing this, I am smiling. This is what it felt like twenty-five years ago. It is still what it feels like today.

Yeah, it sounds too simple and cliché. Even still, I believe that until you know, you don't know. Be yourself. Be patient. Be still. And you will know when you know. Trust me.

FOLLOW THE LEADER

"Maybe God has a bigger plan for me than I had for myself. Like this journey never ends. Like you were sent to me ... to help me through all this. You're my angel."

- A Walk to Remember

What comes to mind when you hear the word *food*?

Immediately, I think of holidays like Easter and Christmas. When I was growing up every holiday was centered around food, like an all-you-can-eat buffet. Well, every day was pretty much centered around food, holiday or not. That's the way my mom rolled.

A year after getting married, I was branded a traitor to the family heritage when I decided to eat a vegetarian diet, limit carbs, and eliminate sugar as much as possible. Immediately after making that change, I noticed a huge difference in my health. I felt lighter from head to toe. My mind was clearer. My energy level increased. I had lived over a quarter century in a sluggish state of diet-induced lethargy, and in just a few days my eyes opened to a whole new state of physical awareness. I felt like Clark Kent entering the phone booth and exiting as Superman. I had put on the cape and discovered I could fly. The foods I had been consuming since I was a child were my kryptonite.

Growing up, eating a lot—of anything—was considered proper nutrition. "What a healthy baby!" Mom would exclaim whenever she saw a newborn shaped like a bowling ball and sporting several rolls on its legs. To her, being healthy meant eating, period. As long as you were eating, you were healthy in her eyes. It didn't matter what you were consuming, either. Food, in any form, equaled health.

Some people can eat whatever they want without any issue. Unfortunately, I'm not one of them, and I had chronic stomach problems and acid reflux for the first two decades of my life. It became so bad in my teenage years that I would sometimes vomit in my sleep. For over a year, I slept on top of a beach towel so my mom wouldn't have to wash my bed sheets every day.

Making a change in eating habits was one big step that helped cure the ailments I lived with for so long.

The initial pushback my wife and I received from others to changing our diet was harsh and confrontational. Our immediate families reacted as if we were condemning their entire way of life because we decided to eat a diet that made us feel better physically. We ended up in arguments over it, once leading to a bag of rice being thrown onto the kitchen floor and someone storming out of our house. I'm telling you, it was crazy!

I did become what you might consider a "health nut." Yeah, one of *those* people. I'm the oddball at the restaurant who asks for a cheeseburger without the cheese and a veggie patty substitute with a side salad. I typically know what I want to order in less than a minute because there are only a handful of things on the menu that I eat; though, nowadays restaurants are expanding their vegetarian and vegan options. In the checkout line at the grocery store, I unload a cart that is eighty percent produce. For years, we ate broccoli for breakfast. That is not an autocorrected typo; we actually ate a bowl of broccoli every morning. As I loaded a few bags of broccoli onto the checkout counter, a clerk once commented, "Wow, somebody's having a broccoli party!" No, just breakfast for the week.

While I had experimented with various methods of eating, I had never tried fasting. I'd heard of some physical and spiritual benefits, but still only thought of fasting as something that people like Ghandi and Jesus practiced. A few days before Easter one year, the idea was tugging at my heart. I had just come out of a very trying season of life, a career change gone bad that I'll share in a later chapter. I'd relied on consistent and intense prayer to get through it, and I was feeling a closer connection to God than ever before. So I wanted to do something special leading up to Easter, something that would connect me closer to the significance of the holiday. That's when it hit me. The Last Supper, recognized on the Thursday before Good Friday, is the start of what we consider a dark moment in history, three days without hope. So I got to thinking, if Jesus went from Thursday night to Sunday without food and his disciples were without hope during that time, perhaps fasting for that same period would be a way to engage in the experience more personally, a little more connected to what the disciples felt while it was happening.

As we approached Maundy Thursday, the idea took root in my heart, but there was one big question that stood in the way: How would this affect my wife and kids? Technically, it shouldn't, but when you're married and have a family, everything you do has the possibility of affecting your spouse. Even just a short, two-and-a-half-day fast. In this scenario, there were a couple factors weighing on my mind.

First, my wife and I were not in the same place spiritually. It felt like I was making significant progress in my faith, growing closer to God, and wanting to increase that momentum. Her faith was by no means waning, but she did not feel that she was in as much of a growth mode. Marriage goes that way. Sometimes one spouse is high and the other low. Sometimes you are moving in the same direction, and other times not. On occasion, the two of you are moving in complete rhythm. We weren't necessarily out of rhythm; we just weren't completely in sync on our faith journey.

There is a very real fear of pursuing personal growth. It's the fear of leaving others behind—your friends, family, or acquaintances. Out of compassion for them and regard for your relationship, the prospect of changing your life and growing apart as a consequence is a scary proposition. It keeps many of us stagnant for periods of our lives, sometimes long periods. In marriage, those consequences are magnified because of the nature of the relationship, and I was sensitive to anything that might cause a wedge between us.

Second, when you have known someone for a while and see all aspects of their behavior—like when you're married and living with your spouse every day—you tend to make predictions of how they will act or react in certain situations. It is a trap that can influence your own behavior or words based on how you foresee the other responding. While consistent patterns of behavior can become somewhat predictable, expecting it can become a self-fulfilling prophecy. It can also cause you to avoid a confrontation altogether.

My wife isn't quite as fanatical about eating habits as I am. I had done some short-term digestive and liver cleanses and had committed to eating as clean as possible at times, and that seemed to put a sense of pressure on her. That pressure might be real or imagined, but it appeared to be a burden of guilt to either participate with me or feel like she wasn't being as "good" as I was with eating habits.

Thinking about telling her that I was going to fast before Easter, I mentally played the reel of her potential reactions. None of them resulted in a positive scene. Fasting for three days was far out of our comfort zones and something that only deeply, very deeply, religious people did (or so it seemed). The last thing I wanted was for her to think that she was being a lesser Christian unless she did it too, or subconsciously resent me for trying to grow closer to God without her. It bothered me enough that I considered not doing it at all, simply to avoid how I thought she would react.

I contemplated, deliberated, then contemplated some more. Ultimately, the decision to do it or not came down to one factor: Priorities. God first, then family. Now, I don't believe following God should lead me away from family. On the contrary, it should bring us closer, or lead them closer to God as well. A former neighbor of ours was a preacher who wound up getting divorced because he spent so much time running the church and trying to feed the church family that he neglected his family at home. God created family first, and without that first family, none of us would be here. If Adam and Eve had focused on work as their priority, regardless of how noble that work might have been, mankind would not have multiplied. Human history would have begun and ended with them. So the concept of putting God first, above family and above a marriage, is not about destroying the marriage in order to follow God's will. It's about our own personal relationship with God and who we are becoming. I knew that the practice of fasting the Friday and Saturday before Easter could potentially make me a better person and a better husband and father. I trust that God will lead me to become my best, most authentic, self—to become every bit the man my wife needs and deserves. That is why I put God first.

The day before Good Friday, I told my wife what I was planning. I would be on a liquid fast in parallel with the time Jesus was arrested in the Garden of Gethsemane to the revelation of his resurrection. Dinner that night would be my last until after church on Easter morning.

Now, I don't mean to brag, but the reaction I had predicted from my wife was spot on.

Her face and body language spoke volumes. At first, she stopped breathing and just stared. This was the "What just happened?" and "What does it mean?" face. Then her breath quickened as her eyes moved up, down, left, and right. This was the "Great, what does this mean for me and the kids ... are we eating by ourselves all weekend?" look. Of course, she didn't say anything out loud initially, so this is all speculation.

After hashing out what this meant for the following few days, it was resolved. I was fasting, they were eating, moving on.

When Friday morning came, I was already in the kitchen, gathering different fruits to make fresh juice for my breakfast, when my wife came downstairs.

"What are you doing?" she asked.

"Making juice for breakfast."

"Will you make some for me? I'm going to fast with you," she said.

And there it was, exactly what I did not want to happen—guilting her into fasting too. The next few minutes was a back-and-forth jabbing match that I had zero chance of winning, but I had to throw a few punches just to make my case.

"Babe, you don't have to do this just because I am."

"I'm not."

"I just want to do something different this year."

"I know."

"Really. You don't have to do this."

"But I want to."

Like I said, the outcome of this debate was predetermined, and one of us had to stop talking or it would have gone on all morning. So, with two freshly made glasses of orange-pineapple-strawberry juice, we started a two-and-a-half-day liquid fast. Together.

If you have ever fasted, you know it is an interesting test of human will. There are a few stages that I typically experience. Beginning a fast is somewhat exciting, knowing that I'm attempting something difficult and meaningful, both physically and mentally. Midway through Day 1, I get hungry, and sometimes a little nauseous. Breathing through it is important, helping to maintain energy and focus. So is staying busy and distracted from the fact that you have no food in your system. By evening, I'm thinking, "Just make it to bedtime, then you can sleep, and you won't have to think about it." The vision of being unconscious throughout the night and not having to worry about feeling hunger pangs is enough motivation to make it through the rest of Day 1 without much problem.

Day 2 can get rough. There is definitely nausea, and the majority of the day is a battle against sluggishness. It is a constant struggle to raise my energy level enough to get through a task, until getting some sustenance with a juice drink for lunch, then continuing to plug away through the afternoon. Focus is literally on one task at a time—get through it, breathe, drink some water, keep going. Bedtime can't come fast enough.

Day 3 is more of a breeze. It's like finishing a 5k run. The first couple miles you might feel all the aches, pains, and difficulty along the way, then you see the finish line in the distance and your whole mindset changes. That's what Day 3 of the fast feels like! A rush of energy hits because you know it is going to be over soon. Very soon. While the second day felt like slugging through a marathon, Day 3 is like a sprint to the end.

That is how it went for our fast leading up to Easter that year. It was a tough, mental test, but we got through it. Having a partner to commiserate with and console was a blessing. We leaned on and supported each other every step of the way.

Easter morning began as a mirror image of Good Friday. I was up first, in the kitchen preparing for the day, when my wife came downstairs. Only a few hours to go. Our first bit of food to break the fast was going to be communion during the morning church service, then we would celebrate with our family at Easter brunch. We both felt a huge sense of accomplishment. We had denied our bodies a basic need and did it for a good purpose. As we hugged and exchanged "good mornings," she looked into my eyes and said, "Thank you for doing this with me."

Did you catch it? Did you recognize what she said and how it differed from the way the experience began? She thanked me for doing it *with her.* How ironic. I was going to do it anyway.

She is the one who did it *with me* and, because she did, I felt so much support and strength and got through it more easily than if I'd done it alone. A few days earlier, I had been afraid to do it because I didn't want her to feel badly or be guilted into doing it too. When it was over, she actually looked at it as something that I did to support *her*. Honestly, I'm not sure how she even came to view it that way. Perhaps it was just a consequence of doing something difficult together, supporting each other, and lifting each other up, regardless of whose idea it was. Whatever the reason, my initial fear of causing a wedge between us by doing this myself was flipped completely around into an experience that brought us closer together.

The moment I decided to commit to this, to put God first, even above my marriage, taught me a profound lesson. No matter how much we go through as a couple or how comfortable we get with each other, we need to keep growing. Keep striving and discovering what it takes to be your best self. It will make you better, might even make your spouse better, and will bring your relationship closer. Some growth opportunities will be together, some will be separate. Don't force it. If you feel the pull to do something hard, to grow, go for it. If not, don't sweat it. Just encourage and support each other to keep striving.

I titled this chapter "Follow the Leader" because the leader in this moment, and in our entire story as a couple, is God. We follow him. He leads us to become better and raises our marriage to heights we cannot get to on our own strength and knowledge. By following him in this moment instead of giving in to the fear that was causing me to doubt how my marriage would be affected, we were both led through a memorable experience and to a tradition that we have continued every Easter since.

As your marriage progresses, keep going. Keep growing. Keep becoming the best version of yourself. Your spouse will benefit from it as much or more than you do.

PERSONAL REFLECTION

OBJECTIVE

To know who you are (the good, bad, and ugly), what you stand for, what you want, and who you want to become. Grab a journal or answer the questions in the space below.

SECTION I: WHO ARE YOU?

What are your deepest core convictions about life and about yourself?

_____

_____

_____

What do you believe in and why do you believe it?

_____

_____

_____

What do you care about? What do you despise?

_____

_____

_____

What type of life do you want to live and uphold? How would
you want to be described?

_____

_____

_____

SECTION II: ABOUT YOUR CURRENT OR PAST RELATIONSHIPS

Why did you enter them? What was your goal or purpose? What
did you primarily want out of them?

_____

_____

_____

What did you do or say regularly to nourish those relationships?
Why did you do or say those things?

_____

_____

_____

Did you or have you done or said anything hurtful? What were the motives behind those behaviors?

_____

_____

_____

Did you alter your behavior or actions to appease the other person?

_____

_____

_____

SECTION III: IF YOU ARE CURRENTLY MARRIED OR IN A RELATIONSHIP

Are there any areas of the relationship in which you feel held back?

_____

_____

_____

Why do you feel this way? Is it because of something external, or is it because of an internal belief?

_____

_____

_____

Are you holding your spouse or significant other back in any way? Why?

_____

_____

_____

SECTION IV: IF YOU ARE CURRENTLY SINGLE

Have you attached any bit of your self-worth to attracting the opposite sex and/or being in a relationship? Be honest.

_____

_____

_____

If you answer "Yes" to the previous question, what is a new belief that you will live by from now on?

_____

_____

_____

What are the most important things you want to know about someone else before you "date" them?

_____

_____

_____

ACTIVITIES

Write down things you do and thoughts you have that are incongruent with who you truly are, how you want to grow, and who you want to become.

_____

_____

_____

If you are married or in a relationship, share this with your significant other.

CHALLENGE

Resolve to live as the person you are and want to become! This week, do something that you don't typically do and that reflects the type of person you want to be.

ACT II, PART 1

BECOMING WE

TWO TO ONE

"Let's be real clear about what we're after here ... The five players on the floor function as one single unit. Team, team, team. Right? No one more important than the other."

  - Hoosiers

A team is a group of individuals working together to achieve a goal. Before my wife and I met on the tennis court, we were individuals, working on our own personal skills to become the best singles players we could. Driving back from our spring break time in Tampa, we realized that our singles careers were about to be over. We knew that our future was calling us to a major shift— the mixed doubles tour, no longer battling alone, but combining forces on the court of life to face our opponents together.

As with any transition from an individual to a team sport or activity, there are some new strategies to learn and implement. On the tennis court, you have to learn different positioning, since you are sharing space with your partner and are no longer required to cover the entire court by yourself. It is actually a detriment to the team if you try to guard the whole court on your own— you'll expend more energy than necessary, leave spots open for your opponent to exploit, and potentially rely on a weakness that might be your partner's strength. You have to learn to manage your space, trust your partner to manage his/hers, and utilize each other's strengths as much as possible. There are times when you serve, and other times when you volley. The concept of the sport and the skills used for it remain the same, but how you play the game together is very different than playing it alone.

Before officially hanging up my tennis shoes on the singles tour, I wanted to get rid of some old baggage, some unfinished business with an opponent I had yet to conquer.

I had a mountain of credit card debt that seemed unfair to bring into a new partnership. It was from a period in my rebellious past, not truly indicative of who I was and the kind of person I wanted to be. From the time I was a youngster through high school, I had the dubious distinction of being the stingiest member of my family. "Cheap" is the word my relatives used. I rarely bought anything other than packs of baseball cards at the local convenience store. I started developing a love for money at an early age, at least, a love for watching money accumulate. Saving money is good. Loving and hoarding it selfishly, not so much. "No one can serve two masters," the Bible says. "Either you will hate the one and love the other, or you will be devoted to the one and despise the other. You cannot serve both God and money" (Matthew 6:24).

College changed me in a lot of ways. How I spent money was one of them. My freshman year, everyone was signing up for credit cards. Who wouldn't be allured by the temptation of buying stuff that you didn't have to pay for?

When the balance on a credit card gets into the thousands, spending another hundred or two doesn't seem like a big deal.

After all, it only adds a few dollars to the monthly payment. In what seemed like the blink of an eye, my credit card debt ballooned, but I was forward thinking. "When I graduate, I'm going to make so much money, none of this current spending is going to matter because I'll be able to pay it off with ease." Of course, that didn't happen right away. The debt just kept growing.

I faced the dilemma of a mountain of credit and the impending entrance into a lifelong partnership with the woman I loved. It would have been unfair of me to burden her with such a large financial liability of mine. The most prudent and noble thing to do was to pay it all off before we tied the knot. I told her I wanted to wait to get married until I was personally debt free. Then I'd be all hers.

It did not take long for one thing to become very clear: the numbers were going to make getting married any time soon very difficult. I'm a numbers guy. I grew up memorizing baseball statistics and learned division by calculating batting averages in my head. Looking at the credit card balance I had at the time compared to my salary and living expenses, I knew there was no way I could afford to pay off the debt in, say, a couple years. Maybe longer. How could I ask her to wait that long to get married? I couldn't. Not if I wanted to avoid putting needless strain on the relationship.

My eyes were also opened to the realization that, by wanting to clear all past debts before moving forward, I was trying too hard to control the conception of our marriage, thinking that we needed to start it without any blemishes. That could actually serve as a detriment—trying to start in a place of perfection, believing that is how it should always be. What will happen when the imperfections show up? Because they will. How will we react? Will we be able to handle the messiness, or will we try to get everything back to perfection as quickly as possible? What happens if we can't handle it?

So it was settled. I was convinced that it would be better to get married with the debt rather than waiting a potentially long, unknown amount of time until the debt was paid off. We were going to get married. Only, I didn't tell her that.

"Why not?" you ask.

Well, deciding to take the next step in our relationship presented another issue, one that required more time, and already having the debt excuse was an excellent distraction.

Though I had surrendered the notion of having a perfect beginning to our marriage, there was one thing I still wanted to be perfect—the proposal. I wanted it to be romantic, emotional, unexpected, and in a beautiful setting. To pull that off, I had to keep delaying, even though we had already resolved that our union was inevitable. Consequently, I stuck to the story that I wouldn't get married until all my financial debt was paid off, and it became just that—a story. It was a fib, a lie, deception for a good reason, I think. However, having to repeat that story weekly became wearisome.

"If we know that we are going to get married, then why wait?" she argued, over and over. Good point. I had no answer other than "Because I want to pay off my debt first." The contradiction inside of me was agonizing. I kept telling her that I wanted to wait, but I didn't want to wait. I just wanted the proposal to be memorable.

We volleyed back and forth for a few months. Every time she lobbed the ball of doubt over the net, I just hit it right back at her, hoping to keep the game going long enough to figure out the right situation to pop the question. We had a fairly even match of groundstrokes back and forth, but the intensity picked up over time. She gained strength and was hitting the ball harder and harder, and it was getting more difficult to defend my territory. Until, without warning, she rushed the net and caught me completely off guard!

"I have enough money saved. What if I pay off your credit card balance for you?"

Uh, oh. I just lost my only viable excuse to keep waiting. I still need more time to set up a proper proposal. I can't believe she's doing this to me! Those were my first thoughts. She was about to smash a winning volley against the only shot I had left in my bag.

Wait. What did she just say? She offered to use *her* own money that she had worked for and earned, to pay off *my* debt. Debt that I had accumulated before she and I ever met. Whoa. She was willing to wipe that debt clean, just so I could feel better about ridding myself of it before she and I started our life together. It was unimaginable. Overwhelming. It was profound, selfless, and loving. It was representative of everything a marriage should be.

In a sense, she beat me to the proposal. She didn't say the words, "Will you marry me," but the question she asked solidified her intent for us and presented me with an opportunity to respond with the same sentiment.

"When we get married, the debt won't be just yours anymore," she said. "It'll be ours. So, let's pay it off and save the interest." She had no hesitation. What most people would consider an entirely senseless and unnecessary solution to my problem was perfectly natural and logical to her. No romantic scenarios I could dream up or arrange could rival the gesture she had just extended. Shortly thereafter, in a rather staged and failed attempt at a memorable proposal that I will share later, we officially got engaged. Game. Set. Match.

By offering to use her own hard-earned savings to pay off my debt, she was not only removing a potential barrier to getting engaged but she was also setting the standard for how we view our union. Nothing is our own anymore. What is hers is mine, and mine hers. It is all *ours,* the assets and the liabilities. There is no longer just me and you, but us. No longer two, but one. What happens to one, impacts both.

With this frame of mind, we dissolved our individual bank accounts when we got married and opened one joint checking account—the same account with the same bank that we still have today. I don't understand the concept of married couples having separate bank accounts. Perhaps individual savings accounts can be held by each so they can surprise each other with gifts, but that can leave room for unhealthy actions or habits to sneak into the marriage. Likewise, if your primary strategy for showing love and affection to your spouse is to buy him or her material things, you might be heading down a slippery slope, not paying attention to the things that matter most. Things like time, attention, caring, understanding, support, and a host of other expressions of love that have nothing to do with buying stuff. Furthermore, if there is something you want to buy for yourself that is so expensive you'd prefer your spouse not know the cost, you shouldn't make the decision to purchase it without his or her input anyway.

Though we've never had individual accounts, even savings accounts, we've been able to surprise each other with not only gifts but also a host of other things that matter even more. Romantic dinners, personal cards and notes, self-created scavenger hunts, breakfast in bed, and intangible things like patience, humility, and just showing up and being there. Those are acts of love that take much more effort than a simple purchase, no matter how expensive it is. They take an investment of the heart and a sacrifice of our most precious asset—time.

The idea of combining our stuff, living our lives as one rather than two, extends well beyond financial considerations. We make many of our decisions, and all of the most important ones, as a team, from the perspective of our partnership. Early on, for example, we were both convicted that our family would be stronger and more prosperous over time if one of us was a full-time parent to our children when they were young. It didn't matter which one of us worked more and who stayed home with the kids. We approached it as a team, and whatever made the most sense and gave the biggest benefit for the team would be how we divided our time and primary roles. We also arranged our service and ministry ambitions as a collective unit. In years when I was more focused on career growth, my wife volunteered more time at church and in our kids' classrooms at school. When the tables eventually turned as the kids got older, the opposite occurred.

We don't view ourselves purely as individuals. My time is not solely my own. It must first be considered in the context of the marriage, the team, before seeking what I want as an individual. While this perspective might seem constrictive at first, it opens up a whole new world of possibilities that aren't available otherwise.

Often in a marriage, it can feel like we are working against each other or that our spouse is holding us back from reaching our greatest potential. *If only I had the freedom to do whatever I wanted,* we might think to ourselves, *there would be boundless time to explore endless opportunities.* That thought is deceiving, and it's a trap. We need to remember when we were single we had the same seemingly unlimited time, and we spent much of it looking for a partner. We tend to view marriage more like an anchor than a sail. However, we don't get married simply to anchor ourselves to one port for the rest of our lives; we get married to double our sails and capture more of the tailwind so we can explore and experience more than we can on our own, and become much more in the process.

Ecclesiastes 4:12 says, "Though one may be overpowered, two can defend themselves. A cord of three strands is not quickly broken." Simply put, we are stronger together. We all know this, but we get sucked into working against each other by a combination of our selfish nature and our forgetting why we joined forces. There is much more to experience in life by doing it together. Two are greater than one. Three is greater still. In our marriage, my wife and I are two, and we look to God as the third strand. That combination of three is not easily broken.

There is a saying, popularized in a movie I like a lot, that I fear has become a perpetuated lie. It was cemented in a monologue at the end of *Jerry Maguire,* when the lead character is pouring out his heart to his estranged wife. He concludes a declaration of his committed love to her with the sentimental statement, "You complete me."

It sounds so good, doesn't it? Enough to give you chills. It is such a concise, snappy line full of emotion, romance, sensitivity, and passion. It is a proclamation that anyone would gush over hearing. Unfortunately, it is a bold-faced lie.

Many of us buy into this lie when we are single and looking for a meaningful relationship. I did once. I believed I was a lesser man when I did not have a steady girlfriend and that having a girlfriend would fulfill an empty part of my life that I could not satisfy on my own. That perspective leads to dependency on another person to complete what is perceived as an empty part of you, a part you have no control over. It relinquishes control to another, so they can make you into the most complete version of yourself. But it is a false premise, and if this is what you believe, you need to reframe that belief. Let me introduce you to the truth about relationships.

You don't complete me.

We complete *us*.

As individuals with God's guidance, we are complete on our own. It goes back to the process in Act I, that we must be our truest, most authentic selves first in order for someone else to love who we really are. I believe that God is our Completer, our Author, and our Perfector. He is the only one who completes us as individuals; no one else on earth can. We cannot fall into the trap of thinking that we are incomplete on our own and need the help of someone else to become a complete person. Thus, on our own, we are complete. Together, we become something more. We become us.

Take our bank accounts as an example. When we had separate accounts before getting married, whatever we had in each account was a complete total, a full amount of our cash balance. There was nothing missing, no gap that needed to be filled. We may have wanted them to be larger amounts (who doesn't?), but it was a complete reflection of what we individually had accumulated up to that point. When we got married and combined accounts, the collective amounts became more, greater than they were on their own. See, we don't complete each other as individuals, we become more together.

Similarly, a singles tennis player is just that already, a tennis player. Adding a doubles partner doesn't transform them from a non-player to a player. It's a different type of game altogether. A team is established that is much more formidable than any one individual player. Combining talents, they work together to become the best they can be as a pair, honing both their individual skills and their collective teamwork, all for the benefit of the partnership on the court.

That is precisely how my wife and I view our marriage. We are not individuals, but a team. We don't complete each other; we help each other become more. We work together for the success of our marriage, our family, and the greater good. We complete us.

EVERYTHING YOU WILL EVER WANT

"I dream about you. Because it's always you."

- *Avengers: Endgame*

I had just stepped into the sanctuary and walked past the front pew where my family was sitting. I glanced over and locked on a short stare with my grandmother. My grandfather was too ill to make the trip to attend. He had gone into the hospital two years earlier with a bad case of pneumonia and came out in a much weaker body. He would battle emphysema the remainder of his life. I wanted to give my grandmother something that she could take back to him, so I smiled and offered a wink that said, *I love you.* She smiled back. *I love you too.*

I took my place at the front of the aisle, and time lingered. Questions ran through my mind, as I waited for the doors to open at the other end and I would see my bride for the first time since the night before. What is she going to look like? How am I going to react? Am I going to burst into tears, or throw up?

"Just stay on your feet," I told myself.

Suddenly, I had a surreal, spiritual experience. I looked around and realized that everyone else in the church had frozen, and I was standing in a still silence. There was no movement or sound. If I had looked at the clock, it probably had stopped ticking as well. It was eerie, but in a good way. It was a moment of clarity. A sense of wholeness and peace. I gazed down the aisle as if peering into the future. Then a soft voice spoke unexpectedly in my head. It was so direct and real, it bordered on being audible.

It said, "Everything you will ever want is right at home."

Where did it come from, and what did it mean? It was not an original thought of my own, that's for sure. I was tired, queasy, and mostly focused on trying not to fall over. A deep thought like that was the furthest thing from my mind, and my head was so cloudy, I don't think I could have conjured it up even if I wanted to. Was God telling me something? Maybe. But what?

The next few seconds were drawn out as I meditated on what those words meant for me now and in the future. Suddenly, I was no longer standing in front of the altar at the church; I was being transported years, decades, into the future. I was watching our marriage on fast-forward. I didn't see specific occurrences, only concepts, but the message was evident. There will be difficulties and disagreements. There will be frustrations and temptations. Through the ups and the downs, the good and the bad, remember this truth and always come back to it: She is everything you will ever want.

At the last supper, when Jesus broke the bread with his disciples, he said, "Do this in remembrance of me." Why did he say that? Why then? Aside from the metaphor of the bread and wine being his body and blood, he was giving them an anchor to remember him by. We forget about things over time. Memories fade. Experiences are diminished. After a long period of time, beliefs we might have once felt strongly about tend to lose their luster. However, if the disciples made sure to remember Jesus *every time* they ate and passed that remembrance and tradition on to others who then passed it on as well, eventually two thousand years later we might remember just as if we were sitting at the table with him. Jesus was giving them an easy way to remember him forever, and I think that's what the voice I heard was doing as well. It was telling me to remember what I was feeling in that moment because it was an eternal truth. Whatever was to come, keep believing in what you know you have right now. She is everything if you choose her to be.

The word "everything" wasn't all-encompassing. It didn't mean every possible thing in life. I still have my own dreams, goals, and desires. There is a lot to explore and experience individually in this world. The voice was speaking to my upcoming marriage, and it was talking about everything in relation to it. The word "home" meant *her*. All the love I will ever want from a woman is with her. All the joy and fulfillment I will ever want in a relationship is with her. Everything, with her.

At that very moment, I was wrapped in wedded bliss. It felt perfect, and that is what we typically remember about the courting and dating stages. We tend to forget how difficult relationships are at first. Is she interested? Does he like me? Should I ask her on a date? Is it going to work? Where is this going? Figuring out each other and the relationship is a heavy load. What gets us through it? A goal. We want something, and when a passionate ambition convicts our hearts, we will bust through any wall to get it. We focus on the outcome and keep running until we get there. On our wedding day, it can seem as if we have run the race and reached the finish line. We have achieved the goal we set out to accomplish. However, that couldn't be further from the truth. The relationship leading up to our wedding day is just pre-race preparation. The marriage is the race itself.

If we believe that our wedding is an accomplishment in itself, a finish line of sorts, we can fall victim to getting too comfortable. When we are too comfortable, challenges feel and become more difficult than they actually are or should be. Any athlete who has made it to the top will say that winning a second championship is more difficult than winning the first. Two things happen when we reach the peak.

One, we've worked hard for a long time and have finally satisfied the burning desire to win. A natural letdown ensues. The urgency and drive to push through all obstacles, no matter how painful, diminishes.

Two, a target is now on our back, and adversaries shoot for it with all their might, every day and every week. We get hit with the best the opposition can bring.

Marriage is no different. The wedding is an end to a former way of life and the beginning of a new one. When we say, "I do," we aren't signing up for unlimited bliss without effort. We are committing to give maximum effort for the bliss we and our partner want to have. Upon sealing the relationship with a kiss, the biggest challenges have yet to begin, and if we believe otherwise, we are setting ourselves up for disappointment and discouragement. From that point on, the world conspires against our marriages, with the goal of breaking them down and tearing us apart. Things like financial strain, sexual temptation, and even children (among many others) present challenges to maintaining a committed, loving relationship in marriage. Approximately half of all marriages end in divorce; do we need any more proof that we have become a people ill-equipped to defeat the opposition that rages against committed relationships?

When I make an honest assessment of my marriage, I acknowledge a lot of flaws and inadequacies in it. We don't communicate as directly or as often as we should. Just like all couples, we get frustrated with each other. There are aspects of her personality that annoy me, and I know there are many more of mine that annoy her. We've made a lot of mistakes, both together and separately. We have said things to each other that hurt, mostly unintentional, but painful nonetheless. In all of our shortcomings and failure, what is it that makes us unique? Why is our relationship so solid, and our love for and commitment to each other stronger now than ever before? I'm sure there are a lot of reasons. This book includes some of them, but if I were to pinpoint one thing that serves as the bedrock, it is our faith in what God said to me before I saw her walk down the aisle.

I believed the Voice I heard when I was standing at the altar. I think we *must* believe it. When time stood still in that moment, I foresaw not only that we would face challenges throughout our marriage but also that there might even be times when it wouldn't *seem* like what was at home was what I still wanted. Without directly saying it, the Voice implied that these times, no matter how lengthy or fleeting, intense or mild, would be deceiving. *If you ever believe that something, anything, is better than what you have at home, you are either being lied to or are lying to yourself. It simply will not be true.* That's what I believe the message was. I decided in that moment to accept what I had heard and believe that everything I will ever want or need will always be right at home. It has been an unwavering conviction, a personal creed for the last two and a half decades.

To be clear, I am not saying that if "home" is a mess, if my marriage is in shambles, that I should want it just as it is. On the contrary, if what I have does not appear to be what I want, then something needs to be fixed, and repairing whatever is broken will get it back to what it needs to be and back to what we want it be.

It is the same concept as the grass on the other side of the fence. If your neighbor's grass is greener than the one in your own yard, it doesn't mean you can never get green grass again. It means you need to water it, tend to it, and care for it until it becomes green. Sometimes it only takes a little work, sometimes it takes a lot. My wife and I have been living in our current house for fifteen years and, as I am writing this book, our lawn is the greenest and thickest it has ever been. There have been years when our lawn was more like the infield of a baseball diamond. There have been years when it was overrun by weeds. There have been years when grass grew in some spots, but not others. Regardless of what condition it was in, I always yearned for a thick green lawn. I just needed to figure out the right strategies to get it that way. We didn't sell our house and move to a new one that had a great lawn already established. We tended to our own, year after year, making it better and better. Just like our marriage, it now looks great to the eye, but there are still blemishes that we want to fix. We're just going to keep going and getting closer to perfection, covering one bare spot at a time.

Certain things in life are non-negotiable. Things that are going to happen no matter what. Aging is an example. Death of loved ones is another. There are other circumstances that we know will pop up—like disappointment, failure, mistakes, and heartbreak.

It is best to decide how we are going to react in those situations and what we are going to believe about them *before* they happen, to help us get through them as emotionally empowered as possible. Emotions can be wonderful sensations, but often make lousy guides when left unchecked. So, standing at the altar, when I heard that Voice imparting lasting wisdom before the most galvanizing moment of my life, I decided in advance, before even knowing what challenges were ahead of us, to believe what it said.

This gets back to the notion that we have to take the concept of marriage more seriously at an early age. We have to do a better job of training up our children to understand its significance—both the blessings and consequences. In traditional wedding vows, we do not pledge to be true and faithful as long as we are happy and marriage is exactly how we want it to be. Unfortunately, that is how we tend to treat it much of the time. As long as it is in a good place and we are satisfied, we are all in. When it gets tough, we justify rebellious or bad behavior. We violate the vows we took.

Several years into our marriage, my wife and I were at a production of *The Nutcracker* ballet and had a conversation with a young amateur dancer in her early twenties. We were approaching our ten-year anniversary and got on the subject of relationships and marriage. We talked about the ups and downs and what makes marriage both difficult and special.

"I've heard that, at some point in the first ten years, every couple considers getting out of their marriage," the young girl asserted.

My wife and I looked at each other with equally dumbfounded expressions. Huh? How about that for a future vision of marriage?

"We haven't," we both said. Not even close. "Getting out" has never been a consideration. It is not an option with us and never has been. Maybe most couples do have that thought. Not us.

Ultimately, getting and staying married is about a choice. Commitment is a choice. Perseverance is a choice. Happiness is a choice. To love or not to love is a choice. It is a choice that both people in a relationship need to make. One cannot choose for the other. None of it is easy, but it still all comes down to choice.

When we recite our vows to each other, we aren't choosing whether or not to go through bad times. Those are inevitable. That's why we declare our allegiance to each other as a covenantal commitment to love all the way through. The choice is to go through, to make the absolute best of it all, to grow together and love each other in spite of the bad times, knowing there is more good to come.

There is a legend of a Spanish conquistador named Hernan Cortes, who in 1519 led a fleet of ships in an attempt to conquer an island off the coast of South America—an island that had been deemed unconquerable. Severely outmanned and outgunned, their odds for success were seven thousand to one. When they arrived on the island, Cortes gathered his men and issued a single, firm order. Knowing that their only chance to conquer the island was if their lives depended on it, he told his men, "Burn the boats." In an act of desperate measure, they burned their own ships and were left with two potential outcomes: take the island, or die trying. Cortes and his men proceeded to take the island!

We need a similar conviction when it comes to marriage— where success is the only option, and we "burn the boats" that might lure us to any solution other than whatever it takes to make it work.

"Everything you will ever want is at home." If we can embrace that and believe it with all our heart, why would we even consider getting *out* of a marriage, if everything we could ever want is *in* it?

GIVE AND RECEIVE

"The most important thing in life is to learn how to give out love, and to let it come in."

- Tuesdays With Morrie

Throughout the continual changes of life, fluctuating plans, and evolving dreams, how do we make sure that everything we will ever want remains at home? How do we not only maintain but grow the love and connection we had in the beginning to unleash a thriving marriage that exceeds our wildest expectations? The answer for us wasn't exactly a particular moment, but a prolonged season during our marriage that led to an illumination.

A couple years into our marriage, I had been toiling with the desire to write a book. I had started one but gave up after a few short months. It was a far too laborious and tedious process for my lack of patience. (I know, the irony.) That experience, however, jump-started what has become a lifelong hobby of writing screenplays. I have written about a dozen. One ended up making the rounds through Hollywood, earning me meetings with a top production company for Sony Studios, as well as Adam Sandler's Happy Madison Productions and Billy Crystal's Face

Productions. Eventually, they all passed on the screenplay, but a potential writing career had momentum.

About the time I was hobnobbing with Los Angeles movie elites, we decided to relocate from the suburbs of Atlanta to the suburbs of Nashville, Tennessee. In conjunction with the move, we made a decision together that I would go all in to pursue a writing career. We then had our second child and went over a year without either of us earning a paycheck. We didn't care much at first. It was the best of both worlds; I chased a dream and, predominantly writing at home, was there to help with the newborn. It was a win-win.

After striking out in Hollywood, I met an aspiring producer right in Nashville who had an idea and needed a writer. The project was a love story, and the purpose was to show an audience the meaning of true love. This would become my writing focus for the next few years and would teach me about true love that transformed and perhaps secured the marriage my wife and I have today.

Before writing a word of the script, we spent months researching the foundational principles of love. To show what love looks like to an audience, we had to define it and know it. We spent countless hours discussing and reflecting on the nature of love. The result was a revelation of an ancient truth and the exposure of a modern lie.

THE TRUTH

Love is not passive, it is active. I don't necessarily believe in the concept of "falling" in love. That is a passive notion which would seem to simply happen *to* you, rather than something you must pursue with intentional effort. A passage in chapter 13 of

1 Corinthians, often read during wedding ceremonies, describes love as being patient, kind, not envious or boastful, not proud or dishonoring, not easily angered, but rejoicing with the truth, always protecting, trusting, hoping, and persevering. This passage is commonly known as one of the most complete pictures of love, which is why so many couples want it as one of their readings at their wedding. Two things stand out with this description:

1. All the words used are verbs. Love is not just a feeling toward someone else; it is the way you treat them, how you act and behave.
2. It makes no mention of getting anything for oneself. It only mentions what actions love gives or doesn't give, each having a direct or indirect impact on people around us in a positive way.

In a word, to love means to *give*.

When we are patient, we give our time and bear circumstances with calm and without grumbling. When we are kind, we give others respect and sympathy. When we do not envy, we give praise and admiration for the success of others. When we are not boastful or proud, we hold back the giving of praise to ourselves and arrogance toward others. Instead, we show humility. By not dishonoring others, we give them grace. When we are not self-seeking, we give selflessly. By not giving in to anger or keeping a record of wrongs, we extend peace and forgiveness. By protecting, trusting, hoping, and persevering, we provide security, belief, faith, and continuous effort, never giving up.

As my eyes were opened to the realization that love is a reflection of what we give of ourselves rather than merely a feeling we experience, I began to see how much my wife had given since we had been married. Over all the years I had spent writing and chasing a dream, her support never wavered. Through childbirth and midnight feedings, the raising and caring for our kids, and the time I spent away from them working and writing long hours, she just kept giving me what I needed to pursue what I wanted. She was patient over the years it took to see results from my efforts, and faithful when I reached dead ends. She never praised herself for being the rock and glue that sustained our family or harped on mistakes and missteps I made along the way. She always trusted that God would guide the way, ever hopeful in the present, and persevering toward a brighter future. I often left the house before she awoke in the morning and worked late into the night after she'd gone to sleep. I could be tired and cranky, constantly seeking time to follow my own passion. She kept giving me that time, day after day, year after year. Her steadfast support is what helped me get through rejection after rejection and keep me going one failure after another.

THE LIE

If the truth is that love is an act of giving, what is the lie we discovered? There is a common belief that marriage is "give and take." That it is "50-50." I'm here to tell you, that is a complete misconception.

A subtle but profound shift in perspective changes everything. The most important lesson to learn about marriage is that it is neither 50-50 nor give and take. It is *100-100*. It is *give and receive*.

First, think about what it means to give and take. We can probably all agree that giving to another person is a positive action. Now, consider the word "take." Think about *taking* something from someone else. Better yet, think about someone else taking something from you. Does it conjure a positive or negative emotion? It could be either. We can take our lover's hand, take a chance, a bath, a vacation, a breath, or a stand. However, taking from someone else has a predominantly negative connotation. I envision grabbing something from their hand, something they might not necessarily want to give up. It could even be done with aggression, pulling it away from them. It might lead to a struggle over the thing being taken and animosity toward the taker. It could even lead to a far worse consequence. How much strain might that put on the relationship?

If we simply change the word *take* to the word *receive* we get an entirely different picture, with the same outcome. When we receive, we are accepting something that is being given to us. It could be the same as the thing we want to take, but we are acquiring it in a much different way.

Think about it visually. Giving is a movement toward something. Therefore, when spouses are giving to each other, they are moving toward each other. They are getting closer together.

$$\male \rightarrow \leftarrow \female$$

In contrast, taking is a movement that pulls something away from another. Therefore, if a spouse is taking from the other, or if both are taking at the same time, they are metaphorically moving away from each other. They are going in opposite directions, pulling apart.

$$\male \leftarrow \rightarrow \female$$

If marriage is 50-50, and half the time we are giving, and half the time we are taking, is it any wonder why half of our marriages are ending in divorce?

You might say that separation only occurs when both are taking at the same time. While true, a sustainable marriage requires both spouses to be moving in concert. If one is predominantly giving, and the other mostly taking, then it becomes a situation of one chasing after the other.

They won't reach a connection point, because one is consistently moving toward and the other moving away.

So how do we ever get what we want if we are consistently focused on giving to our spouse? Therein lies the secret—that marriage should not be 50-50 but 100-100. If we are focused on giving one hundred percent to each other, we should never feel the need to take anything. All, or most of, our needs can be fulfilled by the other.

When we think selfishly and have the 50-50 give and take perspective of marriage, what we *take* is limited to our own wants and desires. The ceiling for what we get out of the marriage only goes as high as what we create in our own minds, the minimum amount that we believe we need or deserve. However, what if we reverse that thinking and, instead, are willing to *receive* whatever our partner gives, and what they give is one hundred percent? What if our partner wants to give *more* than our needs and desires? The ceiling gets lifted, and the possibilities are limitless. The marriage experience becomes more than we ever envisioned.

The other side of giving is the willingness to receive. We should not be so focused on giving one hundred percent of ourselves that we fail to accept what our spouse wants to give to us. It would be like turning down a gift into which someone else has put time, effort, and resources. We must humble ourselves enough to focus primarily on giving to each other and be equally humble to receive from each other.

You may be thinking, "I'm supposed to give one hundred percent to my spouse for the rest of my life?" Yes. While it can seem overwhelming and appear daunting, look at it from the perspective of building a business. When Steve Jobs was creating the concept for Apple, he and his team worked sixteen- to eighteen-hour days in his garage. He got up early, stayed up late, and gave everything he had, every day, for years. They did it because they saw the possible reward for their efforts. Eventually, all the hard work, all that he gave to the business, paid off … big time. At that point, did he stop giving to the business? Did he sit back and just collect the fruits of the effort he had already put into it? No. He kept giving to it, because the greatest reward was in the process, in the continued building of the business to new and greater heights, no matter how high the ceiling of success became. Even after a fallout with his partners that led to his leaving the company he had founded, he eventually came back and gave more to it than he ever had before, raising its impact in our lives to new heights.

The mindset of building a thriving marriage is not much different than building a successful business. It takes consistent effort, every day. From Matthew 6:34, Jesus said, "Therefore, do not worry about tomorrow, for tomorrow will worry about itself. Each day has enough trouble of its own." Do not worry about giving all of yourself for the next fifty years of marriage. Just focus on today, giving what your spouse needs now. Be present in the current moment, and tomorrow will take care of itself. In the preceding verse, he says, "But seek first his kingdom and his righteousness, and all these things will be given to you as well." If we seek first to give, we will be given all these things—our needs, wants, greatest desires, and beyond. This takes focus, discipline, and love of the process—knowing that the desired result will come.

Taking one step at a time while running a marathon. It takes faith, hope, and trust—the groundwork for the resolve to never give up.

Upon realizing this, I decided to test the concept of giving one hundred percent by making it my primary focus for one day.

That particular day, I was asked by my boss to travel to Alabama to help transition another company we were acquiring. The day started bright and early and was filled with a high-stakes deadline and impossible problems to solve.

When the work was finally complete, I was physically and mentally spent. Then I had a three-hour drive home. Two thoughts ran through my mind during that ride: 1) I can't wait to get into bed. 2) If I have anything left, I must give it to my wife when I get home.

Really, I just wanted to get home and go to sleep. But I knew the test wasn't over until I'd given all I could to my wife.

Secretly hoping she would be asleep, I pulled into the driveway and could see the light in our upstairs bedroom still on. Did I have anything at all left to give to her, even if it was just one percent more? I had to find out.

As I walked into the kitchen, there she was in her pajamas. The kids were asleep. She was wrapping up her own long day. Wanting to head straight upstairs and climb into bed, I noticed she was looking at the grocery list. The trek upstairs to bed was going to have to wait.

For years, we have planned our meals a week at a time. We

keep a running list of grocery needs on a magnetic pad that sticks to our refrigerator door. My wife has a peculiar need to review the list with me, as if my confirmation or approval is worth anything. It could also just be a reason to communicate. Whatever the motive is, I stood in the kitchen, focused more on keeping my eyes open and staying on my feet than the list she was reading off and explanations she was giving for why we needed each item. There was no thought of disputing anything she was saying. I just nodded in agreement. Though I really did not care what was on the list that night, I stayed patient and listened to it all.

Eventually, we got through the list and headed upstairs to bed. When I finally laid down, sinking into the mattress, I was in paradise. Exhausted in every sense, having given everything I had, there was not an ounce left to give. As soon as I closed my eyes, the day would be over.

Except, it wasn't over yet. She rolled over onto her side, facing me, in the "pillow talk" posture. Warning! Eyes, remain open! Repeat, do not close the eyelids yet!

She did not realize how tired I was, and I tried not to show it. She wanted to tell me about a dilemma that had been on her mind, about a family member. I just kept telling myself, "If you have anything left to give, give it." I lasted as long as I could before starting to lose the battle. She noticed such heavy-laden eyelids and graciously turned out the light.

Sometimes, we push ourselves physically to see how far we can go and how much we can get out of ourselves. That day was an emotional push from the moment I awoke until I fell right to sleep. It was pushing my heart to see how much I could give to my wife, even after feeling as though I had spent all the energy I had.

Giving all of ourselves can be seen over a season, as my wife exemplified during my writing journey, or a day, like the one I just described. I have been trying to live up to the standard of that day ever since. Some days I am successful; most days I am not. But we should never stop trying. We give until we can give no more.

The revelation that marriage is 100-100 works, and we should have known it works because it is an instruction as ancient as days. Unfortunately, it has been misinterpreted and distorted, causing us to believe in the lie that marriage is give and take and 50-50. The book of Ephesians, in chapter 5, shares a description of how the relationship between a husband and wife is best designed. There is a lot of consternation about these verses but, in proper context, they provide the essence of what naturally makes a successful marriage and life together. *(See the Appendix at the end of this book for a breakdown of this passage and how it relates to us today.)*

As I described in Act I of our story, it is important to first know and be your most authentic self, while continuing to grow into who you are. This is necessary in order to give yourself fully to another. If we don't love who we are and who we are becoming, we will be hesitant to give that version of ourselves completely to someone else. However, if we love ourselves, are grateful and thankful for who we are and what we have, we will freely give it away as a gift to be shared.

Likewise, in order to have one hundred percent of ourselves to give, we must first believe that we are full and complete without our spouse. This is why the notion that "You complete me" is dangerous and false. No one completes us aside from God. Once we recognize and accept that and love ourselves because of it, we can then enhance our experience with another person and create something new—one flesh—that is greater than we are on our own.

The profound mystery of two becoming one flesh cannot happen if the two remain selfish or self-focused. For instance, we cannot become one with water unless we fully submerge ourselves in the pool. If we sit on the edge, dangling our feet to remain mostly dry while still feeling *part* of the water, we will never become one with it. We cannot learn to swim unless we enter it, fully submerged, completely submitted, engulfed by it. The same is true for marriage. Unless we fully submerge ourselves in it, willing to give up everything we have to it and to our spouse, we will not reap the rewards of knowing what it is like and being able to swim through it.

It took my wife and I several years to realize what ultimately makes a marriage thrive. I was recently asking myself: What has made us so great together? How have we managed to successfully avoid the pitfalls and major ups and downs throughout our marriage? We have so many shortcomings as a couple. We have made mistakes, at least I know I have. Some have been huge and have directly or indirectly hurt her. Even still, with all the challenges we have had within and outside of our relationship, we have maintained a fairly smooth ride that just keeps getting better. Why is that?

Posing that question to my wife, we came to the same conclusion. We are consistently striving to decrease our own selfish nature and instead focus on giving to each other. That is the honest answer, and it has worked for us and is what our relationship has always been about. It has helped us build what we have today and what keeps us building still higher. We don't carry negative emotions toward each other to the next day, even if we don't resolve them together right away. The giving, unselfish mindset does not allow us to remain in frustration, anger, or discontent very long. We not only give, we also forgive. If something happens between us one day, we just move right on into the next day and start giving to each other again.

For example, before the COVID-19 pandemic in 2020, when our lives were running like a well-oiled machine, I made dinner every night so she could work longer, and she cleaned up the kitchen afterward. It was a system that worked well. During the pandemic, however, we both experienced a significant increase in workload, but the expectation about dinner seemed to never change. We did not effectively communicate alternative options, we just kept on doing what we had been doing. So, when supper time came and went throughout the week and both of us were still mired in our work, guess who defaulted to dinner duty? I did, just as I had before. *I'm just as busy, if not busier than her,* I would think to myself. *If it wasn't for me, we'd either be eating at midnight, or we wouldn't eat at all.* It was frustrating to experience (our fault), and I failed to communicate those frustrations effectively (my fault). Those moments of frustration would quickly dissipate for a few reasons:

1. I realized that if I wasn't going to communicate them, I had no right to hold onto them.
2. I knew that, eventually, everything would balance out. For years, my wife sacrificed her time in exactly the same way. Not that this was a form of payback, but I trusted and had faith that it all evens out.
3. If I really didn't want to make dinner, we could order out or have something that was very quick to prepare.
4. Once dinner was over and cleaned up, I much preferred

to spend close time together, sometimes snuggling on the couch to a show on Netflix, rather than to continue being frustrated about who did what. So we just moved on.

She acts the same way toward me. I have had many days, sometimes one after the other, when I have felt overwhelmed and stressed, and I showed it by behaving sarcastically, short, and cranky. If I were her, I'd let myself have an earful of scolding. Most of the time, she doesn't, unless my behavior crosses a line or borders on becoming destructive to our relationship. She understands, moves on, and treats the next day anew.

We have many of the same challenges that all couples have, but we rarely let them carry on to the next day because we are consistently focused on giving to each other and to the marriage. It has allowed us to get away with mistakes, shortcomings, and challenges. Realizing how we tick, we can work on fixing the things that we don't do well and look forward to a relationship that will get even better!

Learning the important lesson of giving—that it is the foundation of a loving marriage—was a strength we would rely on to face trials that were to come. The dream of being a professional screenwriter did not materialize—at least, not yet. It has been a fun, exhilarating, and terrifying ride. After all those years of dedication and sacrifice toward that goal, it was our marriage that was growing and becoming stronger than ever. In the end, there is nothing greater that we could ask for.

MOMENT #9

A KNIGHT'S TALE

"Listen to me, mister. You're my knight in shining armor. Don't forget it."

- *On Golden Pond*

I remember only one time when I was angry with my wife. It hit me at the most inopportune moment and threatened to prevent one of the most magical experiences of our life together.

Growing up, there were few things my wife was more passionate about than dancing. Her parents once showed me an old VHS tape from her high school years. She was dancing in a local production of *The Nutcracker*. I'd known that she had danced since she was a toddler and was dedicated to the rigorous and countless hours of practice, enduring strict instruction and relentless pounding on her body. However, watching that tape was the first time I had seen her dance. I stared at the grainy television screen, mesmerized by her beauty, fluidity, strength, and gracefulness. She was good, very good. She was better at dancing than I had ever been at anything I had ever done.

Approaching her mid-thirties, more than a decade and a half since she had last danced, she would periodically comment about how much she missed it. "It is never too late to be what you might have been," a quote attributed to George Eliot, had become a motto of ours. Not that professional dancing was in her future, but perhaps just dancing again was, and should be. The idea had come up enough for us to decide that whenever we had the slightest discretionary income (since we had none for years), she would look at taking a dance class again. As if we spoke it into existence, God took the words and started laying out a plan.

While my first job in Nashville did not pay enough to cover all our monthly expenses, my next job provided a significant salary increase, and it was enough to start looking for a house to buy. We found one right in the neighborhood we hoped to live in, before the property had even been listed on the market. We met the owners, toured it, liked it, and bought it.

The wife who owned the house we purchased ran a dance studio in town and, of course, encouraged my wife to take lessons. All of a sudden, the idea of her taking lessons again someday became "this is where you need to go." I heard someone say recently that if you simply pay attention to the people God puts in your life, you won't ever have to network. We were paying attention.

Shortly after we moved into our new home, she started taking classes at the former owner's studio. It was an old romance rekindled. (One that I could fully support with no potential repercussions this time.) Finally, after years of parenting and supporting my goals and dreams, she was doing something for herself.

A couple months later, I was flipping through the community newspaper and saw a half-page advertisement for a local production of *The Nutcracker* in historic Franklin, Tennessee, right in our backyard. It was a call to dancers of all ages to audition for the show. How perfect? An opportunity for my wife to enter a portal to the past, to revisit a time when she was free to express herself and be whoever she wanted to be, with dreams and aspirations as big as the whole world. *She can't pass this up,* I thought.

I was home alone at the time. I folded the newspaper so that it was open to the advertisement and placed it on the corner of the kitchen table and wrinkled the pages a little to make it look like it had been plopped there randomly. Subtle! It worked, but not exactly how I had imagined. She came home, saw it, and didn't say a word. She just kept on going through the rest of the evening without showing an inkling of interest.

I was certain this was a destined arrangement. If she got a part in it, great! If not, at least she would know she gave it a shot. Where's the downside? Of course, it is easy to think that way about someone else's opportunity. When it is our own, doubt often shouts in our ear. "What if I audition and don't get a part, basically telling me that dancing is officially in the past? Worse, what if I do get a part, and can't handle the strain?" I imagine there were a few "What if" questions circling in her mind the second her eyes landed on the newspaper advertisement.

I eventually brought it up later that evening, asking if she had seen it, trying to suppress my eagerness. After initially blowing it off, she took some convincing, but she eventually agreed to attend the audition … just to see what would happen.

"Yes!" I bellowed to myself. Not only was she practicing dance for the first time since high school, she was on her way back to the big show!

The morning of the audition came, and I was naively exuberant over the chance of her getting a part in the performance. She, on the other hand, was nervous and unsure—which either she hid very well, or my excitement blinded me from noticing it.

Less than an hour before she was set to leave for the audition, it happened. An attack on the moment. An emotional or spiritual attack … or both. Brought on by a relatively innocent mishap, it nearly derailed this ordained opportunity and everything that was meant to come after it.

I was rummaging around in the kitchen, which opens up to our living room. Our daughter, about a year and a half old at the time, was waddling throughout the living area, when she got behind one of our wing-backed chairs and grabbed ahold of it for stability. In what seemed to play out in slow motion, the chair ever so gently started tipping backward on top of her. I could do nothing but watch it happen from the next room, too far away to run and stop it.

My wife was standing in the living room, a few arm lengths away from our daughter. I waited for my wife to jump over and catch the chair.

Only, she never moved. The chair toppled over, right on our little girl. I rushed over and pulled her out from under it. Thankfully, she was fine. No harm, no foul. Just another scary incident for a parent of a toddler learning her bearings.

Then it hit me. Anger. I shot a glare back at my wife, who was still standing in the same spot, just a couple steps away. She had watched it happen, could have stopped it, but didn't move. *Why would she just stand there?* I wondered. I didn't say anything, but I was livid.

I typically try to process my emotions before reacting, but this felt different. There was no cognitive contemplation; I went from worried to incensed without hesitation. Looking back on it now that fifteen years have passed, was the teetering chair really that big of a deal? At worst, our daughter might have ended up with a bump or a bruise. She certainly wasn't in serious danger. So I was left with two questions: Why didn't my wife try to stop the chair from falling on her, and, at the same time, why did I become so easily angered by what turned out to be a harmless incident?

Realizing the temper flaring up inside me, I dusted my daughter off, sent her on her way, and marched out of the room. My wife was on the verge of a momentous audition, and I was ready to blow my top at her.

The reason I describe this as an attack is because it didn't make logical sense. Why would my wife watch a chair fall on our toddler without moving a muscle or blinking an eye? Natural instinct should have caused her to involuntarily react, not to mention that our daughter was in harm's way. And my anger— there have been many times in my life when an angry response could have been much more excused, but rarely have I felt it as swiftly and strongly as I did then. Not that anger is ever truly justified, but I've had much worse happen to me. What was it about this particular moment that triggered such instantaneous rage? There had to be something else underlying all the emotion.

I looked at the clock. It was nearing time for my wife to leave for the audition, and I was about to explode with something like, "How could you? Don't you care about the safety of your daughter?"

I have to say something, I thought. My wife and I are good at not allowing little things to bother us, but this was different. This required a discussion, if for no other reason than to make sure she knew that it upset me. But when do I say it? And do I even have the willpower to suppress it, or was it just going to come out like a firehose?

Then, I saw a picture of my wife up on stage in the middle of the audition, with a beaten down and broken demeanor, and what had triggered that demeanor was my yelling at her. In the picture, she was not enjoying the audition, was not at her best, and wound up with a negative, adverse experience, ultimately not getting a part and not ever having another chance to dance in a real performance again. It was just a few minutes of auditioning, ruined by what I said and how I said it before she went on the stage.

A thought came to mind that confirmed what I was envisioning. *If you blow your top right now, it is going to ruin her frame of mind as she goes to this audition. You can't do that to her.* The air started to come out of my wrath.

Going back to 1 Corinthians 13, love is "not easily angered" but is "patient" and "kind." A few things became clear in this moment. There would be other times to share my displeasure about what just happened, but there would not be another audition for this performance. That is, I will have other opportunities to do what I wanted to do (yell at her), but she would not have another opportunity to do what she wanted (audition). The success of her audition might very well have hinged on what I gave her in that moment. Would I give her my anger or kindness? The choice was mine.

I resolved that my feelings would have to wait—just until later that night, once the audition was over. I gave myself permission to be as angry and animated as I wanted to be … later. It was the same advice I gave to the boys on the Little League baseball teams I'd coached. Whenever I saw a kid get overly upset and carry that emotion with him for a while, I would take him aside and tell him, "It's okay to be upset. I'd be upset too, if I were you, but here's what I want you to do. Be upset for only ten seconds right now. You can be as upset as you want after the game or later tonight. But right now, you are part of a team, and no matter what just happened, in ten seconds you have another job to do. If you just struck out, in ten seconds you either need to cheer on the next batter or grab your glove and go play your position. If you just made an error in the field, in ten seconds the pitcher is going to throw another pitch, and you need to be ready. You can get back to being upset later."

For the betterment of the team—that is, our marriage—and the benefit of my wife, I gave myself only ten more seconds to be upset, then I moved on because I had another job to do. I needed to be supportive and encouraging. I needed to cheer her on, and help her get into the best mindset possible, because she was about to take her swing, and the game was on the line. So I embraced patience and kindness instead of my anger.

It was not easy, believe me. For the next twenty minutes, it felt as if I were holding my breath the entire time. We didn't say much to each other. I wished her luck and gave her a kiss. She walked out the door, and I let all the air out of my lungs. With the heat of the moment diffused for the time being, there was one more thing I felt the urge to do, to completely step into the spirit of giving and eradicate any emotions that might serve to work against her. I took a few minutes to pray for her audition. On my knees—after making sure God was fully aware that I was going to express my anger to her later—I asked for favor over her.

A few hours later, the phone rang. It was my wife, fighting back tears, struggling to get the words out. She was on her way home. The audition was over. She had gotten a part in the show! My prayer had been answered. She was going to be dancing in

The Nutcracker for the first time since high school. Through tears of joy and gratitude, we finished a wonderful conversation, and I hung up the phone and awaited her arrival home.

Now what? A familiar dilemma presented itself. I had delayed my anger until later, but now later had arrived, and she was so excited and thankful. Again, clarity showed up in the midst of perplexity. If I was to follow through with expressing my emotions from earlier in the day, it would connect a negative experience to the positive of having achieved a role in the show. It would ruin the excitement of the accomplishment. "You can't do that to her, either," the Voice spoke again.

Well, shoot! When was I going to get what I wanted? Not yet. That night needed to be focused on celebrating. That was the whole reason for laying out the newspaper with the advertisement of the audition. It's why I encouraged her to take the chance—for the opportunity to experience a victory like this. So, instead of preparing to give her a scolding, I prepared a romantic dinner. We rejoiced over her accomplishment and looked forward with nervous anticipation to what was to come from it.

Dance practices were every weekend. After the first couple, she came home questioning whether or not she could keep up and sincerely doubting her ability to continue. Her toes were getting bashed, and her body was feeling the strain. She wasn't a teenager anymore. She was a mid-thirties mother of two, dancing with younger girls whose youthful fitness and flexibility caused her to feel totally inadequate. She was out of her league, unable to do what she used to, and it bothered her. It just wasn't the same, not what she had expected or wanted it to be like, and she contemplated quitting before they got too deep into the rehearsals.

I offered my best "Win one for the Gipper" speech, assured her that she's not supposed to be like the younger girls, she just needs to be herself. She stuck with it, one hard week after another, persevering through the pain and imperfection. As the months went by, she grew stronger and more confident and was stepping into a new way of approaching dance.

All the while, we still had not discussed what happened the morning of the audition.

Performance day arrived. She dressed the part and went through routines and rituals as she had so many times before in her life—but something was different. A good different. When she danced all those years as a youth and in high school, she had always seemed to be doing it for other people. Whether it was in competition with her peers or under the enormous demands of her instructor, she never truly danced for herself. This performance was not that way. She was embracing a different side of the dance and of the dancer within. Something special was unfolding.

The performance hall was huge, and a lot of people came to see the show. I was in the front row with my kids, along with my in-laws, sister-in-law, and several other friends and acquaintances who came in support of my wife. After all the doubt, struggles, time, and effort that got my wife and me to this point, I knew the victory had already been won. I also knew that my wife wanted to perform well. It's her nature to strive for perfection, and she's driven to be her best in everything she does.

When the lights dimmed, the music slowly faded in, and the production began, I was brought right back to watching the old, grainy VHS tape of her dancing in high school. You might think I have biased eyes when I say this—okay, maybe I do—but having been to several professional productions of *The Nutcracker*,

I know a good show when I see it. This was good, and so was she. No, she was more than good. She killed it! She was beautiful, graceful, and strong. As far as I could tell, she never faltered, and she had the most gorgeous smile the whole time on stage. It was a triumph unlike anything I had ever witnessed.

Even if I am partial about her performance, where she shined the most didn't even happen on stage. When the show was over and the dancers, still dressed in their costumes, came out to meet the audience, she became larger than life. Our daughter was too young to appreciate it, but our six-year-old son was mesmerized when he saw his momma come out in full costume. He stood by her leg, gazing up at her with an angelic reverence in his eyes while she talked with family and friends. She was a superstar, an idol, and at least for a night, the biggest hero he had ever had.

One by one, other moms, some with their daughters, came to congratulate and marvel at her. She had become an inspiring symbol to them: the dreams they had were not lost, and who they used to be before they were called "Mom" was not gone. Think about it ... she was a mid-thirties mom who hadn't danced in half a lifetime. Most people would have considered that past chapter of their life closed forever, but she decided to open it up and do it again. She even became a role model for some of the younger girls who were there. I saw it on their faces and heard it in their voices when they talked with her.

Perhaps even greater than all of that was seeing her father tear up when he gave her a hug. I have seen him cry twice, once at a funeral when one of his heroes had unexpectedly passed away, and this moment, after watching his adult daughter dance once again. After witnessing a spectacle of such magic and majesty, I understood why the forces of darkness had tried to stop this from ever taking flight the morning of the audition.

Up to this point in the story, I could have become resentful if I didn't understand the power of giving one hundred percent in a marriage. I had given up my pride and frustration from the morning of the audition; had given her all the support she needed to take the initial step and keep going; had given up my Saturdays so she could rehearse and my nights during the week of the performance. I could have been asking, "What's in it for me?" At a previous time in my life, I probably would have been asking that.

However, giving to each other in a marriage isn't always equal all of the time. It ebbs and flows, just like most things in life. We just need to keep giving all of ourselves, ready to receive when the time comes. That night, the satisfaction of watching her succeed, having such a positive impact on family and friends, was more than enough for me. It truly was. But … it wasn't all.

When the smiles, hugs, and jubilation ended and the lights turned off, she and I rode home together. After a long, hectic, and restless week, it was our first opportunity to reflect on the whole experience. I told her how proud I was of her, and she gave me some intimate details that only I was privy to, like what she prayed before taking the stage, and how she broke down in tears of joy and gratitude when she scampered off after the last act. Unlike her dancing experience as a youth, she didn't worry about how great she *needed* to be. She gave the dance, her effort, and the result completely to God. From that, she experienced a joy of dancing that she had never known in all the years she had dedicated to it before. This performance completed her journey as a dancer.

Sitting in the front seat of the car, staring into the dark night up ahead, her eyes welled up as she turned to me and said, "Thank you for being my prince."

And there it was.

All it took was a few minutes of swallowing my pride and anger, and a few months of giving her time to do this for herself, for me to receive the greatest gift I could imagine. After ten years of marriage, two kids, three moves, a year and a half without income, and a myriad of other challenges and blessings, she called me her prince. Is there anything a guy wants more than to be a prince for his princess? We had weathered the storms, defied the obstacles, given everything we had, and now we reaped the rewards. It was a beautiful moment that defined precisely what we wanted our marriage to be like.

"Did you ever talk about what happened the morning of the audition?" you ask. Of course we did … seven months later, strolling the Riverwalk to the Magnificent Mile in Chicago on a summer afternoon. We were there for a friend's wedding, and our conversation as we walked led to discussing the dynamic of relationships, marriage, and, you guessed it, back to the *Nutcracker* journey and the day of the audition. One day had led to another, and, as happens over time, other priorities became consistently more important and the emotions that had been so hot in the moment diminished. On the walk in Chicago, I admitted for the first time how I felt about the incident the morning of the audition and how angry I was at her. "I knew," she said. "I could see it on your face."

Then she told me something that put the whole experience into a different perspective.

"You have no idea how close I was to not going to that audition," she said. She was right, I had no idea. Apparently, that day she was so anxious that she considered skipping the audition altogether. She had actually plotted to leave the house, go sit in a coffee shop for two hours, then come home and tell me she didn't get a part. She was already in such a fragile state. "If you had blown up at me that morning," she said, "there is no way I would have gone to the audition."

How close did we come—did I come—to ruining everything that she, we, and others experienced through her journey that Christmas season? Had I succumbed to my emotions and had she decided not to audition because of it or any other reason, she wouldn't have danced one more time. She wouldn't have been an inspiration to other moms. She wouldn't have been a hero to her son, shared an endearing hug with her father, or felt the joy of the Lord throughout the performance. But she did do all those things. She left an indelible mark on so many people and closed the chapter of her dancing career in a light that gave it more meaning and satisfaction than she would have ever had otherwise. Did all that happen because I decided to be angry for only ten seconds? Maybe so.

Have you ever thought that some emotions might just be triggered by forces outside of yourself? I'm not talking about what someone else might do that causes you to feel a certain way. No one can truly make us feel anything. We choose to allow those feelings to surface. What I mean is a potentially false emotion—like my overreaction to the chair my daughter was pulling down on top of herself. My wife was so anxious about the upcoming audition, so lost in uneasy thought, that she was paralyzed physically. It's not that she didn't want to move and stop the chair; I don't think she could. She was stuck in her own head, frozen with fear, and I nearly destroyed her chance at a redemptive journey because of such a swift anger that I had never before or have since felt toward her. It wasn't logical or rational.

Thankfully, when there are forces working against us, there are also opposite and more powerful forces working for us. The vision and voice that came to me in the heat of the moment, as I fumed in my own cloud of fury, certainly wasn't my own. It was an alternate pathway, another behavior to consider, giving me a clear choice between two reactions. It was up to me to decide which to act upon.

Be aware and mindful of moments in your marriage that matter. Recognize the actions and responses that will have an effect on the long haul. Rather than simply reacting to an emotion, decide to take action that will strengthen your relationship now and for the future. We are going to be tested, and how we respond to those tests will determine the vitality of our relationships. Like pushing ourselves through an exercise or a long run, the tests are there to strengthen our ability to love and to increase our capability to love more deeply.

To be focused and aware when significant moments like this happen means we have to want more. We have to want the future to be better than the present, and we have to believe that it can be.

No, marriage is not like a fairy tale, but why not strive for it? Why not treat each other like a prince and a princess? As a prince, I didn't "rescue" her. In this example, I encouraged, supported, and loved my wife throughout her journey. Perhaps I gave her a little fuel to help her fly, to spread her wings, and to be all that she was created to be. She became a princess all on her own.

Together we became royalty. At least, in each other's eyes ... and that's all that really matters.

PERSONAL REFLECTION

OBJECTIVE
To live as a team in your marriage, not as separate individuals.

SECTION I: ARE YOU LIVING AS ONE OR TWO?
What parts of your marriage are separate that could be combined?

_____

_____

_____

Why are they separate?

_____

_____

_____

Would combining any of these things benefit the marriage?

_____

_____

_____

SECTION II: IS YOUR MARRIAGE GIVE AND TAKE, OR GIVE AND RECEIVE?

What are some things you want that you aren't getting out of the relationship? How can you give those things to each other?

_____

_____

_____

Is there anything that feels like your spouse is "taking" in the relationship? Talk about better ways to obtain this; how you can give it to your spouse instead.

_____

_____

_____

SECTION III: HOW CAN YOU INCREASE YOUR ENCOURAGEMENT TO YOUR SPOUSE?

What are things you are doing for which you would like encouragement and accountability from your spouse?

_____

_____

_____

In what individual pursuits do you want (or need) to involve your spouse?

_____

_____

_____

SECTION IV: IF YOU ARE CURRENTLY SINGLE

What are the most important things you will want out of marriage?

_____

_____

_____

What parts of yourself might you need to change or improve to become the most giving version of yourself?

_____

_____

_____

Are there any parts of your life in which you are guarded?

_____

_____

_____

What would you have to do in order to share that part of your life with someone else?

_____

_____

_____

ACTIVITIES

Set a big goal for you and your spouse to work toward together in the next twelve months. It could be a physical activity, vacation, or event. Something that will be unforgettable that you plan for and work toward together.

CHALLENGE

Spend a day focusing on giving everything you have of yourself to your spouse or significant other. During the normal course of a day, do not expect anything for yourself. Rather, make it a day in which you give more to your spouse or significant other than usual, and the day does not end until you have given your spouse your full effort. Do this on a regular day, not a holiday or special day.

Here are a few examples and suggestions:

» Get up early to do something special before your spouse wakes up, such as fixing breakfast, making lunch for the day, or cleaning the kitchen. Do something unexpected that helps your spouse.

» Leave a card or written note with an endearing message somewhere your spouse will find it.

» Call or text your spouse during the day just to say, "I love you."

» Make dinner.

» Engage in conversation, focusing on your spouse.

PRIORITY

FIRST FAMILY

"A man who doesn't spend time with his family can never be a real man."

- The Godfather

The details are fuzzy, but the image is still vivid. My wife was lying on the living room floor, balled up, sobbing and crying out, "I'm sick of living like this!"

We had just returned home from what was supposed to have been a fun afternoon. One of our cars had broken down ... again.

Coming through the door, my wife walked straight through the kitchen, dropped her purse, and crumpled to the floor. Her body just gave out, overcome by the weight of emotions. I don't remember how long she stayed there. I don't even remember what happened next. The only picture left in my memory is watching her fall to the floor and wondering how much longer she would feel this way.

How much longer would we have to pinch pennies just to get by and secure the necessities of life? Where did I fail her? What did we do wrong? We had put our family first.

We had been living on one income for several years and on no income for some of that time. Early in our marriage, we made a mutual decision that if we had children, one of us would be a stay-at-home-parent until our kids reached elementary school age. It did not matter which one of us it would be, we simply believed that the responsibility of raising our children was ours, and that their initial years of development were critical to establishing relationships and raising them the best we could. After we had our firstborn, I envisioned eighteen to twenty-two years into the future, knowing we had him for that finite period of time, and asked, "What do I want him to be equipped with when he enters adulthood?" I played a game of *Would You Rather* with that vision. When he is twenty years old, would you rather that he have money and unlimited resources, or character and the emotional abilities to accomplish whatever he wants? The answer was obvious: all of the above!

Of course I want my kids to have it all—good character, the cognitive and emotional strength to overcome, as well as the money and resources to provide support and security! Who wouldn't? The question, however, isn't designed to choose one or the other but rather to set priorities.

Much of life is about defining our priorities and deciding whether we will follow them. Every decision we make and action we take is a clarification of our own values or priorities. We do what we value most. What I and my wife value most about our children is their character. Right from the start, we made decisions about how we parented based on who we wanted them to become as adults. If they don't end up with it all—wealth *and* character— if we have at least invested in their character and faith, we will have no regrets.

Prioritizing family over everything else produced three main challenges:

1. Either my wife or I would have to stall a career.
2. Wealth and financial freedom would be more difficult to achieve.
3. Abundant and intentional time with the kids and each other was necessary.

CAREER

My wife had always wanted to be two things: a teacher and a mother. Since my salary was greater than hers when we had our first child, we agreed that she would transition to be the stay-at-home parent. It was a perfect scenario—she would step away from teaching while the kids were little, then go back to working full-time when they reached school age. She and they would be on the same schedule, and I could continue building my career, dream-chasing, or both. On paper, it was a simple choice.

WEALTH AND FINANCES

What does it look like in the twenty-first century for a middle-class family in suburban southeastern America to live on one income while trying to make a dream come true? For starters, it forced us to strip our expenses down to the bone. We looked at everything we spent money on and decided what was truly necessary and what could be reduced or removed.

Being close to Nashville, we were in Dave Ramsey's backyard, and we subscribed to his methods of spending to achieve *Financial Peace,* which we learned about in his book of the same title. His program is simple—you decide how to allocate and spend your salary, then stick to it. No impulse spending. Cash is king; spending is more disciplined when actual money is used versus credit or debit cards. Think about it this way: Before going grocery shopping, you make a grocery list of the bare essentials that you need to get through the week. When you get to the store, if an item is not on the list, it doesn't go in the cart. Period.

To execute on this system, we withdrew cash from our savings account once per month to cover our recurring necessary, and some discretionary, expenses that did not require writing a check (as did utility bills). We divided that cash into marked envelopes for items like Grocery, Restaurant, Haircuts, Entertainment, and Babysitter. We decided how much we were willing and could afford to spend on each of these things every month. If the cash in an envelope ran out before the month ended, we had to figure out how to get through the remaining days on whatever resources we had available, without spending any more money. There were many months when we emptied the kitchen pantry during the last few days to avoid going back to the grocery store. We got creative with simple and cheap meals like rice and beans, pasta, grilled cheese, peanut butter and jelly, cereal ... whatever we could scrape together.

In addition to controlling our standard monthly outlays, we drove the same cheap cars for years. When we relocated to Nashville right before our second child was born, we sold our newest and nicest car, replacing it with a hand-me-down from my wife's parents. They gave us a silver Pontiac Grand Marquis, a stereotypical grandparent land barge. Just days before we moved out of Atlanta, a neighbor backed his car into it, denting the rear door on the driver's side. He begged us not to claim it on insurance and said he would have the door replaced. We obliged, but when we got the car back from the shop, the new door was a different shade of gray than the original. Impatient and short on time, we didn't argue, figuring this was just a short-term transition vehicle until we got to Nashville and would get a new one anyhow. Well, we ended up driving that Grand Marquis with a miscolored door for a few years before getting another hand-me-down from my wife's parents—our first minivan. Yup, we were no longer just young professionals having the time of our lives. We were officially a family. Meanwhile, I drove my wife's fourteen-year-old Honda Accord that she'd had since college, with over two hundred thousand miles on its engine. We were no envy of car enthusiasts.

Vacations were a rarity. We actually didn't take a true vacation until our oldest child was eight years old. Until then, every "vacation" we took was to see family members which, let's face it, isn't really a vacation. We saw my parents once or, if lucky, twice a year, usually around holidays. One year, we even drove the thousand-mile journey up to Massachusetts because it was cheaper than flying. By the time we got back home, we just about needed a vacation from each other after so much time together confined in a car. We'll never do that again.

We finally got tired of those types of vacations and decided to bite the bullet and take a family trip to Disney World. The question was, how to get there and back on our meager budget? I'll tell you how—we planned every step so meticulously that Clark W. Griswold would have been jealous. We left Nashville and made our first stop in Atlanta, staying with a good friend of my wife's, whom she knew from college. The next day, we drove to Tampa and stayed with a cousin of mine. We made peanut butter and jelly sandwiches for the ride and didn't buy anything but gasoline on the way down. My cousins were older and, typical with my parent's generation, didn't allow us to pay for any food while we stayed with them. They had a pleasant little house near the beach with a screened-in pool and a hot tub. It was paradise to us. From there, we drove to Orlando and bunked with an old neighbor. The next morning, we woke bright and early to get to Disney World right when the gates opened for an all-day adventure in the Magic Kingdom. We hit all the main attractions, rode most of the rides we wanted, and covered as much ground as we could on a sweltering midsummer day. By nighttime, we were sweaty and tired but determined to stay for the fireworks show because we were all in and wanted to squeeze every last drop from this one-time excursion. As the sun started going down, however, our five-year-old daughter was falling asleep on my shoulder. She didn't say a thing, but the expression on her face was begging us to take her home. After a long day of laughing and running and sweating and waiting, we left right before the fireworks started. The next day, we got up and drove all the way back home to Nashville. All totaled, we had the time of our young family lives for about a thousand dollars.

After that trip, our youngest child was entering kindergarten, and it was time to execute the next step in our grand plan of balancing parenting and careers. It had been eight years since we earned two incomes and, with both kids about to be in school full time, my wife was free to go back to teaching. Only, when we sat down to talk about it, she clearly wasn't ready to return to working full time, and I couldn't argue. The demands and landscape of teaching had increased in just the few years she was out of it. She would have to learn new skills and upgrade her education to fulfill the requirements of the job. Teaching is no longer a 7:00 a.m. to 3:00 p.m. job with full summers off (if it ever was), and it had changed dramatically even in the few years she took off.

We also discussed what it would do to our family structure for both of us to work full-time. She had taken a part-time job at our church that ended up being more like full-time hours, and it had negatively impacted our home life. Things were not the same within our family during the year and a half she worked for the church, and we were afraid that her working as a full-time teacher while our kids were still in elementary school would upset our family life even more. We had gotten into a nice groove, with me sustaining a career and still chasing a dream as a screenwriter and her working part-time and volunteering both in the kids' classrooms and at church. We didn't want to disrupt that just yet, so the grand master plan would wait one more year. Then it waited another ... and another ... and several more, until our oldest child was in high school and both children were mostly self-sufficient, nearly a decade after we had originally envisioned. Years of scraping by, trimming expenditures as much as we possibly could, and then trimming them some more.

For this prolonged season in our marriage, we went without cable television or smartphones. We also committed the cardinal sin of discontinuing deposits to our retirement accounts; we were simply unable to do so *and* pay our bills. Neither could we afford to start college funds for our kids. We didn't upgrade or replace anything in our house unless we had to—like when the garage door, dryer, and dishwasher broke, all in the same year. We lived with the same furniture for about twenty years, some of which dated back to our college days. We didn't buy new clothes until the current ones wore out, so our wardrobes far outlasted styles and trends.

I have heard many couples say, "We can't afford to live on one income." Yes, you can. Just ask any single mother. If you are someone who believes you can't, I challenge you to be honest with yourself. Stop using the excuse that you can't afford it, and discover the truthful, underlying reasons why you don't think you can make do with only one spouse bringing in a full-time salary. By saying we "can't afford" to live on one income, we are suggesting that we can't afford to eat, clothe, and shelter. Those are the true basics of "living." Instead, if we deep dive into the meaning behind that excuse, what most of us really mean is: We can't afford to live in the kind of house we want to live in. We can't afford to have the kind of car we want to drive. We can't afford to dine at the restaurants we want to eat at. We can't afford to take the vacations we want to take. We can't afford to buy the clothes we want to wear. We can't afford to retire when we want to stop working.

To be fair, many couples can both work full-time and make it all work, and work well, for their entire family. I know several of them who have great families, great kids, and hardly seem to miss a beat. For us, at first, we didn't even want to try to have dual careers while raising children. Then we recognized that we did not function well as a family when both my wife and I were working a lot. I'm not saying my wife and I didn't work hard. We did. We have worked long and hard at everything we've engaged in, whether it has been a job, ministry, volunteering, parenting, or anything else. However, we have always understood our priorities—God, family, work, leisure—and when those priorities got out of balance, we made adjustments to get them back in line.

It was hard for many years, but that's what makes it worth it. We will always place financial stability behind emotional and family stability. The purpose for that may change somewhat as time passes, but the primary reason we chose to live this way for the past two decades is because we have been committed to our family and being intentional parents.

INTENTIONAL PARENTING

A marriage can change dramatically when children are introduced into it, and merely everything about marriage becomes exponentially more difficult. While it is tremendously important to not let our parental responsibilities diminish our spousal relationships, is it possible to use our responsibilities as parents and our relationships with our children to strengthen our marriage?

Before my wife and I ever heard about the concept of "Intentional Parenting," we were practicing it. We knew before we had our first child that we wanted to be very deliberate and purposeful parents. So when our first child came into the world, we were ready! If you are a parent, you can stop rolling your eyes or laughing, because you know that no matter how prepared you try to be, you never get to the point of actually being ready to be a parent. Even if you have a desire to be active and intentional parents, when you eventually become one, you realize that carrying out a plan often becomes secondary to just trying to survive a day.

The demands of parenting make it even more important that we have a plan for intentionality; otherwise, those demands can easily dominate our home life and diminish our marital relationship.

When our children were young, I had a conversation with my mom about how difficult it is to raise kids. I remember she was trying to give me advice, telling me just to do the best I can, making a very clichéd comment: "Unfortunately, there isn't a manual to tell you what to do with them." Actually, there is a ton of resources that can help! Books, workshops, counselors ... people who have found things that work well and from whom we can gain insight and wisdom. Read, listen, and learn. There is help available, we just have to make the effort and try different suggestions until we find what works for us. When our firstborn was barely a toddler, we took a parenting class at our church that helped us set some foundations we continued to build upon.

Raising children is the most important project a married couple will undertake together. As in any business or partnership, we can choose to work at it together, through all the ups and downs, toward a common outcome, or we can simply wing it and get blown around by the daily grind of trying to care for another human being.

Let's face it, children are both the greatest blessing and the biggest hindrance between a husband and wife, but I don't think we see them as such in the beginning. With our first child, we didn't realize how much of a deterrent he would be in our relationship, and for how long! My wife and I were married for three and a half years before we had him. That was three and a half years of just us. We are now in our twentieth year of having children—twenty years of trying to find time to be together, just the two of us. Twenty years of being responsible for other human beings living with us. Having a plan with our kids and being intentional with how we raise them is a critical component of sustaining and strengthening a marital bond.

FAMILY FIRST

The best lesson I ever learned from my mother was not to put money or ego ahead of family. When I was in high school, my extended family split because two people, first cousins my mother's age, had a disagreement over who deserved more money from the sale of a shared business. The adults in our family were essentially forced to choose sides, even the ones who had nothing to do with the dispute. Instantly, my closest cousins, with whom I had shared most of my holidays, vacations, and special moments growing up, were suddenly no longer in my life ... and they haven't been since. In the decades that followed, my mother never held a grudge against anyone on either side. For the next few decades, she never stopped trying to get family members back together. Unfortunately, she had minimal success. Through all the squabbles we had with family members, being together was more important to her than being right and worth more than any amount of money.

That perspective is similar to how my wife and I view putting family first. So often, we say that family is our highest priority in life, but our actions rarely show it. Do our goals and calendars reflect the priorities that we claim to uphold? For most of us, the answer would be "No." That is certainly true for us at times. Putting family first does not mean we prioritize every single family activity or need above everything else in our lives. It means that family is our center. If we cannot do and have it all (though we try, just like everyone else), we make sure that at least our family is the best it can be. Simply put, when we have more than one priority of equal value and significance, family always takes precedence.

When my son was a senior in high school, he was experiencing some heightened emotional situations that he had never dealt with before, and on one particular day, some challenges came to a head. I had received a couple phone calls at work in the middle of the day, informing me what was going on. I didn't know exactly how the events of this day were affecting him, but I knew he might be struggling and alone. So I dropped what I was doing and left work early to spend time with him and make sure he was okay. The work would have to wait because my son was more important. That day, I made it very clear to him that, no matter what else I might have to do—and there was a lot happening at work then—he was more important, and I wouldn't let anything come ahead of him, his sister, or his mother, especially in times like that. He looked up at me with glossy eyes. Family first.

So, husbands love your wives. Wives, love your husbands. Submit all other parts of your lives to prioritize your marriage and family. Parents, be intentional with your children and not just live-in babysitters. Have a larger vision for who you want your children to become, and actively raise them as their guide and teacher throughout their young lives.

Take stock of what you and your family are capable of undertaking. Different couples can handle different levels of responsibility and pressure from work and other extracurricular activities. Be acutely aware of when you have surpassed your own threshold and when you've come to a point that becomes diminishing or destructive to your family. Adjust whatever needs to be adjusted to make sure your family is strong, even if it means other aspects of your life aren't as grandiose as you'd like them to be … yet. Make sure that your family is the strongest pillar of your life, and everything else will fall in line.

This is one of the reasons I decided to write this book. Too many marriages end too quickly. Too many families are torn apart. Too many kids are being raised by single mothers. Too many priorities edge out family. We must wake up and realize that we can make do with less stuff in our lives, but we can't do with less love and support from each other. When we get to the end of our lives, and we all will get there, we won't remember the stuff we lost as much as the relationships. Our spouse and children will not value the material things we gave them more than the time we gave them. I am convinced that if more families will start prioritizing each other with actions and not just words, sticking together and taking care of each other, we will see positive change in our culture, country, and world like never before.

SITTER MONEY

Detective: So, what's your story?

Claire: Just a boring married couple from New Jersey.

- *Date Night*

The most difficult aspect of putting family first is maintaining a proper prioritization within the context of the family itself. When I say "family," I am including children in that equation.

When children enter the world, it is easy to believe that they are the most important priority in your life. They quickly present the most urgent everyday needs. However, within a family, children are not and should not be the highest priority. The marriage should still hold that distinction.

My wife and I put God over everything in our life, so as we look at the dynamic of our family, we want him to be sovereign over all. Under him, our family is the central nucleus, and the core of that nucleus is our marriage. A family cannot be sustained without a stabilized marriage. Put simply, if the core crumbles, the family will fall apart with it.

There is a lot of research that suggests children whose parents love and remain committed to each other are much happier and more secure than children who are raised in a relatively loveless or broken environment. This is why the marriage has to be prioritized over children. That does not mean we should leave our babies to fend for themselves while we constantly work on our marriage. It means we have to intentionally feed the marriage to make sure it is sustained; otherwise, it may starve to death under the demands of parenthood. It is too easy to fall into a pattern of making children the priority all the time.

What happens when children are the priority all the time? There is a great risk of a husband and wife growing apart, which can lead to separation, divorce, and the breaking apart of the family unit. We also teach our children that the world revolves around them, promoting an entitled and selfish character.

What happens when marriage is made the priority? We show our children what a healthy marriage looks like, so they can learn from it and replicate it someday. Seeing their parents' relationship coming first, before their own wants and needs, shows them that others are just as important as they are—and sometimes more so. It helps promote more considerate, more respectful, and less self-absorbed behavior that will serve them well as they grow up.

The question is, how do we prioritize our marriage when it seems that our children demand everything we have in us every single day? Especially while trying to build a career and chase dreams. And on a limited budget. That is precisely the scenario we found ourselves in. What did we do? We stuffed envelopes with cash.

Don't get too dramatic about it; we did it out of necessity to control spending, not because we were flush with monetary wealth. As mentioned earlier, we used Dave Ramsey's method of expense management when I was out of work for fifteen months after moving to Nashville. Since we had no income, we needed a way to control what we spent to make our savings last as long as possible.

When we were first setting up our envelope system, we went through it meticulously, determining the minimum amounts we felt we could live on. One envelope we deliberated over was marked for "Babysitter." This became personal for us. In a time when we searched for any little morsel in the kitchen cupboards to stick to our monthly grocery budget and still try to remain properly nourished, having a Babysitter envelope might not have seemed like a necessity. Unfortunately, we did not have easy access to free childcare. However, if we were going to feed our marriage and make it a priority in the midst of parenthood, periodically getting a babysitter to give us a night out was essential. So we resolved to allocate money to our Babysitter envelope, and use it no matter what! We would eat crackers and peanut butter to stick to our budget if it meant we could go out on a date, just the two of us, at least once a month. The moment we decided that we would always use our babysitter money set a standard that our marriage was more important than money, children, or any circumstance life could throw at us.

We started our monthly Babysitter budget at forty dollars a month. Paying a good, reliable, and trustworthy sitter up to ten dollars an hour gave us four hours of time away from the house without kids. That is about 0.5 percent of an entire month's time. It's not much.

While it provided a vital albeit short time together, it was only the beginning of what we knew our marriage required. In addition to one official date night a month, we had to get creative. We had to make those dates special somehow, to enhance the experience, to really make the time count for something, and we had to find other ways to experience magical moments together. Sometimes we went on cheap dates, just coffee or tea, to stretch our money as much as possible. Other times, well, we thought way out of the box.

For one of our anniversaries, I surprised my wife with a cruise. In our living room. That's right, we sailed the vast ocean within the confines of our 14x12-foot family room. Here's how: I bought two big rolls of cheap plastic covering (like a thin picnic table cover), one powder blue and the other dark blue, and hung them along every inch of our four walls. The powder blue was on the top half, to mimic a clear bright blue sky. The dark blue was the deep ocean on the bottom half, where we cruised as far as our imaginations took us. We spent the night eating and dreaming on our own live-in journey through the high seas.

On other special days, we have sent each other on scavenger hunts. One Valentine's Day, I left work early to set it all up. First, I stopped by a liquor store to buy a bottle of cheap champagne, then a video store (back when they still existed) to rent a romantic movie and a restaurant to buy dessert. I took nothing home with me from those places, instead leaving all of them at their retail locations for my wife to pick up. Her quest began with a riddle, the answer to which led her to the first destination, where she was met with another riddle to solve that took her to the next location, and so on. The final clue led her back home, straight upstairs to an already drawn bubble bath with a glass of champagne on the side, while I busily finished fixing dinner. The total cost of the adventure was a few grocery items, movie rental, inexpensive champagne, and some thought and effort. The return on that investment was an enchanting moment and a memory that lasted.

When our budgeted allotments for restaurant and babysitter ran out for the month, we set up our own dinner dates at home. This was one of our favorite rendezvous because it also got our children involved.

We have a round decorative table, just big enough for two, that we set up in the middle of the living room, complete with a single rose centerpiece and lighted candles. We employed our children to be our servers, and they really played the part! Picture a seven-year-old and a four-year-old dressed in their Sunday best, showing us to our seats and handing us printed menus.

They had their own tiny pads where they would write our drink orders—usually water, tea, or lemonade—then head into the kitchen to pour them, plate our food, and deliver it all to our table. They would ask if we needed anything else, then head upstairs where they would have their own dinner and watch a movie by themselves. I am not sure if it was more precious or priceless, but it was definitely some of both. We ended up with a dinner and a movie date without having to leave the house and spend any extra money. Involving our children made it special for all of us.

For cheap entertainment and something to share together after the kids went to bed, we watched the entire series of the hit television show *Lost* on Netflix. If you are not familiar with the show, it is essentially about a group of people stranded on an island. For the series grand finale, we set up beach chairs in our living room, dressed up in our beach clothes (in late winter), and blended pina coladas. We made the simple act of watching television an event.

The decision to always use our babysitter money, no matter what financial struggles we went through, set a standard for our marriage that continues to this day. As my salary increased over time, we added to our sitter allowance little by little, giving us more options to spend precious and necessary time together to communicate, decompress, connect, and experience life. That time should not be taken for granted and cannot be compromised.

We must make marriage a priority and feed it regularly, lest it wilt under everyday pressure and demands. Even if you do not have children and making time together may be easier, you still have to nourish the relationship with planned, spontaneous, and creative time together. Do not let the ease or challenge of your circumstances tempt you into diminishing or putting that off.

Regardless of how good or grueling your situation in life is, endure it together. I would rather walk through a valley with my wife than stand on a mountain top alone. Whether you are in a valley, on the peak, or somewhere in between, make memories together. They could be adventures to the ends of the earth or dinner dates one room over from your toddlers. Do what you can with what you have and where you are. The key is to do it!

RENEWAL

"I vow to fiercely love you in all your forms, now and forever. I promise to never forget that this is a once in a lifetime love. And to always know in the deepest part of my soul that no matter what challenges might carry us apart, we will always find our way back to each other."

- The Vow

My wife and I were recently rebaptized, during our twenty-fourth year of marriage. We didn't do it with much fanfare. No special dinner or celebration afterwards. We didn't even tell people we were doing it, including our own families.

The church we had started attending in the middle of the COVID-19 pandemic had set up a pool where they performed baptisms every week when the services concluded. The number of people baptized each week varied in number. It was simple; we got in line, climbed into the pool, got dunked, and got out of the water to be greeted by someone with a warm towel. It wasn't a spectacle. We simply wanted to renew our commitment to the Christian lifestyle we try to uphold.

Renewal is a regular part of our society. We renew licenses, memberships, subscriptions, and contracts. Every now and then, why not renew other more important aspects of our lives, like our commitment to God ... and our marriages?

My wife and I decided early on to do this. The idea sparked in 1999, after attending a mass in Chiesa dei Santi Pietro e Paolo, a Catholic Church set in a small piazza of Torri Del Benaco, Italy. How we got there in the first place was a renewing of our minds in itself.

A year earlier, we were having dinner in an Italian restaurant, talking about how great it would be to visit Italy someday. My family has a long history of talking about doing things "someday." My grandparents talked for years about visiting Italy, but it would take my grandmother overcoming a dreadful fear of flying and getting on an airplane for the first time in her life in order to get there. My parents dreamed of seeing the "old country" as well, but now in the latter part of their lives, never had. It seemed that everyone in my family was destined to vacation in Italy *someday*, including me—until I realized that there are only seven days in a week, and *someday* is not one of them.

Sitting in that restaurant, surrounded by authentic Italian cuisine and ambience, we asked ourselves, "Why not us? Why not now? Why wait?"

The initial reasons to wait were obvious—people like us don't spend a lot of money or take expensive vacations until everything else in life is accomplished and secured. But what if we did? If we didn't do it then, maybe no one in our family ever would. Whatever the trip would cost might be far outweighed by the experience and what we could bring back to our families at home. To them, it might be like us taking a voyage to the moon and bringing back artifacts from a whole different world. That is how eccentric a trip like this was viewed in my family.

So we resolved that we would be the ones to board the rocket ship and cross the great divide into the unknown. It was a recalibrating, a renewing of our old habitual thoughts, breaking through limiting beliefs that might have held us back before.

A year later, we were sitting in the small Catholic church of the town where my great-grandparents originated. We were trying to figure out how to drop a few dollars into the offering basket that was being passed around. I had already reached for the basket twice to no avail as it just kept going back and forth in front of us. I started to think that they didn't want our money, until an older Italian gentleman sitting at the end of our pew in the back of the church gave a soft whistle and a nod at me. Ah, now it was my turn. Apparently, he had seen my previous unsuccessful attempts. There was something familiar about him—the faint whistle, nod, and ever so slight half smile—all the mannerisms of my own grandfather, as if he were sent there to give us a bit of guidance in the town of my ancestors.

We were in Torri Del Benaco, a small town in northern Italy located on Lago di Garda, the largest lake in the country. It is approximately forty-five minutes from Verona. For the eight days we stayed there, our eyes were opened to the possibilities and dreams we didn't realistically explore prior to the trip.

We toured Verona, the setting of Shakespeare's classic tragedy *Romeo and Juliet*.

We also took a day trip to Venice, where there was one destination at the top of our to-do list—Harry's Bar. Before leaving the states, my mother reminded me (several times) that a drink with our namesake, the Peach Bellini, was invented at Harry's Bar. She also made sure I was aware that "Nicole Kidman loves to drink Peach Bellinis at Harry's Bar in Venice." I have no idea why that was important. "Great, Mom, I'll make sure to say hello if we see her."

Unfortunately, we did not realize that Harry's Bar is not your typical bar, at least as you would picture it if you're coming from small-town USA. When I think of a bar, I see a small, dimly lit, smoke-filled dive with a jukebox in the corner playing old music. Harry's Bar, on the other hand, is an upscale restaurant that serves fifty-dollar hamburgers. In hindsight, I should have realized that Nicole Kidman wouldn't hang out in a dive.

Regardless, we got there and walked in, ready to order our Peach Bellinis. We were immediately met by the maître d' and informed that we could not stay.

"I'm sorry, there is a dress code." We were wearing shorts and t-shirts and carrying backpacks, looking like sightseers drifting through Europe.

We traveled halfway across the world to drink a cocktail with our last name on it, in the bar that invented it, and we couldn't even get in the door. I wish I had pulled out my driver's license, showed them my name, and begged them for one drink, even in a to-go cup, if they offer such common fair. But I didn't. "Is Nicole here? My mom wants me to say hi!" That wouldn't have worked, either.

We left with our backpacks between our legs and no drinks. The next day, however, we had an experience with a Bellini that made a drink at Harry's Bar seem entirely insignificant.

While we were in Venice, a gentleman we had met, who was a distant relative of my dad's cousin, took a walk through the town to see if he could find anyone named Bellini. To our amazement and elation, he found a woman in her eighties who had never married, living on the same quaint piazza as the church we had attended earlier in the week. Her name was Francesca Bellini.

We met Francesca outside her home, an old sailor's lodge from half a lifetime ago. She exhibited the same mannerisms that the elders in my family had—the way she crossed her arms, held her body tight and spoke softly, with a stoic expression. We shared our family tree. Her eyes widened, then she got up from her chair, shuffled into her building, and returned with a picture of an older, stately-looking man, encased in a stone frame. It was a photograph of my great-grandfather. He was her uncle. Turns out, Francesca was my grandfather's first cousin. Her eyes teared up as she handed us the photograph. After talking a little while longer, she gave us a vintage bottle of wine from her shelf, with the stipulation that we open it with my grandfather. How could we not oblige?

On our last night in Italy, my wife and I were walking through that same piazza, reflecting on all we had experienced on the trip and particularly in that magical setting. On one side of the piazza was the building where we had chatted with Francesca, on the other was a pizzeria owned by another distant family cousin. A minute's walk away was beautiful Lake Garda, flanked by a backdrop of majestic mountains, where the sunrise showed its splendor as I had never seen it before. In the middle of it all was the small church.

As we stood there, relishing the moment, we were two weeks away from celebrating our second wedding anniversary, and an idea sparked in both of us. What if we returned to that same spot for our ten-year anniversary and renewed our vows in that very church? What if we brought our close family members with us? It would be a dream come true for everyone. At that time in our life, money was of no consequence. We were young, building our careers, childless, and invincible. We expected to be independently wealthy by our tenth year of marriage and would love nothing more than to treat our family to the trip of a lifetime. The goal was set. For our ten-year wedding anniversary, we were going to celebrate in Italy with a renewal of our vows in Chiesa dei Santi Pietro e Paolo.

The next eight years drifted us further from that vision than we could ever have imagined. Our financial status not only stopped improving, it took a significant downturn instead. Over that time, as mentioned previously, we quit both our jobs, had two children, moved three times, and spent a year and a half without income. Going back to Italy, never mind bringing anyone else with us, had become a fleeting, distant aspiration. In fact, it never even came up again.

That does not mean we had forgotten about it. As we approached our ten-year milestone, I reflected on that dreamy scenario. Inside, I felt like a failure as a husband. Our inability to afford the trip we had imagined was just a symptom of the prolonged financial difficulties we were enduring. We were living the opposite life that we had hoped and prayed for, but remember this—never let your circumstances keep you from realizing your dreams, even if you have to create them differently than you originally envisioned.

Though we couldn't do exactly what we wanted and how we wanted, we had to do something memorable to commemorate our first decade together. So, just as we had learned to be creative with our envelope system of budgeting, it was time to think outside the box for a celebration we could remember forever.

We didn't go to Italy. We brought Italy to us! I spent weeks planning, scheming, and organizing a surprise that my wife would hopefully never forget.

On the day of our anniversary, I scheduled a massage for her that came with a facial and hair styling. The works. That was supposed to be her gift. She thought she was going to the massage parlor, coming home, and spending a quiet night with just me. However, the key to a good surprise is the same as pulling off a magic trick—the art of misdirection. What you are told to focus on is just a decoy; the real trick is always happening somewhere else.

When the massage experience was over, her matron of honor showed up at the parlor with a bouquet of flowers and a fancy dress for her to change into. She was taking my wife to an undisclosed location.

My wife had no idea what to expect until they pulled into the parking lot of our church. Gathered there was a small group of immediate family and close friends. They were waiting in the sanctuary for her to arrive, as if it were our wedding day all over again. This time, I took the opportunity to make amends for one of the biggest mistakes I made early on in our marriage—the proposal.

Ten years earlier, after successfully delaying the question, waiting for the perfect moment, I rather imperfectly carried it out, leading to a near disaster. We were on vacation in Martha's Vineyard, with dinner reservations at a restaurant on the beach our first night there. A dream setting, right? Not quite.

On the way to the restaurant, we were having a playful conversation, when out of nowhere she laughed and, oddly, slapped my right thigh. *Why would she do that? Does she know?* Thankfully, the ring was in my other pocket, so the plan wasn't given away completely. She was clearly fishing, and the element of surprise was losing its luster. Strike one.

After dinner, I awkwardly coerced her to wander down the boardwalk to the pier overlooking the ocean. When we arrived at the dock, I pulled the ring out of my pocket, moved behind her, wrapped my arms around her waist, and held the ring out in front of her. She was completely unaware and just continued with the conversation we were having. After a few seconds that felt like an hour, she finally looked down, noticed the ring, and jerked with nervous excitement. She grabbed for it, knocked it out of my fingers, and we both gasped, watching it fall to the floor of the pier. In a split second, months of preparation and a few thousand dollars were about to fall through the planks into the dark abyss beneath our feet. Strike two.

We heard the ring bounce and she stooped down to see it lying on the floorboard. A near disaster averted. She picked it up, put it on her finger, turned to me for an embrace, and it was over. Only, what my wife remembers most about that night is something that never happened. After all the trickery performed and facades played for weeks in order to get to a perfectly romantic destination, to flawlessly execute a legendary proposal, not only did I fumble through every step, I missed the one thing she cared about most. I didn't get down on my knee. Strike three.

Ten years later, as she was traipsing down the outdoor walkway toward us, I met her before she got to the sanctuary, got down on one knee, and asked, "Will you marry me again?" It may not have completely made up for the initial mishap, but it was special nonetheless.

In a small ceremony led by our senior pastor, we renewed our vows in front of God and our close friends and family.

After the brief service, part two of the surprise unfolded. Back at our house, a celebration was being assembled. Many of our friends were awaiting our arrival for an Italian party. We had plates, napkins, and cups in the colors of Italy's national flag. Italian beer was chilling on ice. Yes, Peach Bellinis were mixed and ready to pour. We even had the ultimate Italian food—cheese and pepperoni pizza!

It was perfect. Our dream of doing this back in Italy having fallen through might have been the biggest blessing we could have received. Being home, we were able to celebrate with so many more of our friends and family. And rather than paying more attention to the extravaganza of traveling abroad, we focused on the most important piece of it all, renewing our vows. It took even more effort, creativity, and sacrifice to pull off. In many ways, it was a more meaningful moment than had it happened in Torri del Benaco.

I urge all married couples to renew the vows that you took on your wedding day. Do it at least once; do it every year if you want to. The circumstances of our lives change many times from the day we initially recite those vows, taking us to peaks and through valleys. People change over time, including ourselves and our spouses. What does not need to change is the covenant we make with each other. That is the only way to make it through the difficulties and heartaches of a life spent in union.

When my wife and I reached our ten-year anniversary, we were not the same couple who stood in the piazza of Torri del Benaco. Our outlook on life was a little different. Our vision had changed. Our relationship and family were different, as was our situation in life. Growth and experience do that to all of us.

On our wedding day, we thought we were at the height of our

relationship, with our whole life ahead of us without a blemish. After ten years together and all we had done through the good, bad, and worse, we looked at each other and declared that we were just getting started. It was an important affirmation. It was important to refresh our relationship and renew the same vow based on who we had become and what our life was like in that moment.

It is important to show each other and ourselves that we are committed in all times, for richer or poorer, better or worse. Sometimes, it is good to remind each other that no matter what, we will go through life together. That is what we wanted and committed to when we got engaged, and no trial or triumph can change that without our permission. Renewing and recommitting to that covenant at a very different and much more challenging stage of life was powerful.

It made our bond stronger than ever. It was a promise to reinvent our marriage to become everything we wanted it to be. Little did we know, we were about to enter another frightening season and would have to rely on that promise to get through it.

MOMENT #13

THROUGH THE VALLEY

John: Why do you find it so hard to believe?
Jack: Why do you find it so easy?
John: It's never been easy!

- Lost, Season 2, Episode 3

The summer we celebrated our ten-year anniversary was during a troubling and tumultuous season of our life that was bubbling toward a startling conclusion. It had all begun two summers earlier when I got my first job after we had moved to Tennessee. The salary was *almost* as much as our bare-bones monthly expenses, but it was enough to keep us afloat.

A year later, I received a call out of the blue from a recruiter about a potential job opportunity with a truck leasing company. It was an accounting position that held the title of CFO. Don't be too impressed. The title was much more glamorous than the job.

The company's office was on Music Row in Nashville, in the heart of the country music industry. I was hooked from the moment I got the interview. "We have access to plenty of cash," one of the owners told me during the interview. "Cash is not a problem." The picture he painted was of a booming business model and growth prospects they were having difficulty quantifying. They needed someone to work the numbers and organize the cash flow. I was their man.

Within a couple months, I had started this new job at a significant salary increase, was writing a screenplay in partnership with an aspiring film producer, and my wife and I had closed on a house, finally planting some permanent roots in Tennessee. We were on a winning streak, looking forward to what God had planned for us next.

Over the first few months in the new job, warning signs started popping up. There were very few filters on language and behavior in the office—not exactly my style, but it was a jovial group who spoke freely and directly. The guy in charge of running the company, with whom I had interviewed, liked to play video solitaire more than he worked. They had no idea whatsoever how much the equipment they sold was ultimately costing them or what prices they needed to charge to ensure a margin. The line of credit, or "cash" as the part-owner had referred to it in my interview, was going to run out in just a few months because of the massive hemorrhaging on their books. *Cash* was going to become an enormous problem without a drastic change.

Then I noticed a few trucks on the books that were not generating any revenue. They appeared to be sunk costs, but I couldn't figure out why, or where they were.

"Those trucks don't exist," I was told. Huh? We had invoices for them. "We created those invoices so the bank would let us draw from the line of credit, but we never bought the trucks. We used that money to pay repair costs on other trucks instead."

So, let me get this straight … fake invoices were created to dupe the bank into giving out money to buy trucks that didn't exist because the company needed the money to pay expenses. This was much worse than I had originally thought. They weren't just bad businessmen; they were committing bank fraud!

Quitting was on my mind, but how far would that set our family back? How long would it take to find work again? On the other hand, by staying at the company, would I be complicit in any illegalities they were engaged in, even if I didn't participate in them myself? I wanted to provide for my wife and kids, but not without upholding our morals and integrity. We were in a difficult spot, and I did not know the right answer.

A couple truths hit us right away. First, I was willing to do whatever "we" felt was best. Though it was my job and my reputation on the line, whatever I decided to do would impact our whole family—so it wasn't just about me. It needed to be a collective decision that both of us agreed upon. Second, we both felt that I should not make a rash decision. Rather, I would take whatever time was necessary to determine the best path, or at least the right one. No knee-jerk reactions. We would take some time to evaluate and discern.

So we prayed. We prayed separately, we prayed together, and through those prayers, we acquired a peace about what action to take. I felt that I was put in that job for a reason. To help influence. To help the people find a better way for the company. They were good people without direction.

Then, again in prayer, I heard this, "When it is time, I will take you out of there." If I was truly led to that job, then why not rely on that same guidance to lead me out of it? My wife and I agreed I would stay. I would help influence change while also looking for another job, believing that God would lead me in the right direction.

In hindsight, was this the best way to approach the predicament I was in? I don't know. I'm not even sure I would advise someone else in the same situation to do what I did. However, my wife and I agreed on this plan and had a collective peace in following it.

The next few months were emotionally taxing. I spent most of it working up business models that would lead the company out of debt, while watching the leaders continue the same behaviors that had gotten them into the mess in the first place. It was easy to see the rapid downward spiral and eventual crash landing that was coming unless things changed quickly. I read and prayed Psalm 91 regularly. It is a staple in scary times, and I leaned on its promises heavily, believing in the protection it assures.

For so long, it seemed as if the leaders of the company were blind to the impending doom. Then, out of the blue, they woke from their slumber. Something had finally clicked, and their eyes were opened. One day in late August, all employees were called into the conference room and given an ultimatum—dedicate the next several months of our lives to do whatever it takes to turn the company around, or leave.

It was a stark contrast to the interview I'd had with them over a year earlier when I heard that "Cash is not a problem." There was a heaviness in the room. It made me uneasy. The big, lazy, solitaire-playing teddy bear of a boss who hired me was shooting fire from his eyes and daggers from his mouth. He demanded that we dedicate our lives to the company for at least the rest of the year, and if we weren't willing to do that, we had twenty-four hours to let them know. "I don't care what you have going on in your personal lives," he exclaimed. "This is your main priority."

It is difficult to explain, but there was an aura in the room that I have never felt before or since. I'm not sure if it was a bully tactic or straight malevolence. I had anticipated this day would come, but not how it ended up playing out.

I left the office after lunch and went straight to our church. I walked into the sanctuary, stepped up to the altar, and knelt. I was all alone. Having no idea how long I would be there, I resolved to stay until I received a peaceful answer to the worrisome dilemma that I was in. I went over potential scenarios in my mind—what our family might have to endure if I quit, what mud I could get dragged through if I stayed. I toiled with my thoughts and pleaded to God for quite a while. He began to answer.

"I told you, when it is time, I will get you out of there," is what I heard again. Was it not time yet? How would I know when it was time? Was I supposed to just stay and watch them drive the company into the ground or wait for something bad to happen to me?

Tremendous peace and calm came over me, though. When that happens, I know I am on the right path. So I got up, took the tranquility with me, went home, and discussed it with my wife. She agreed completely. Family first. I was not going to dedicate my life to their cause for any period of time if they were not willing to change the behaviors that created the problem. I had personal values and standards that I was unwilling to set down, but I would not abandon them in their hour of greatest need.

The next morning, I went into work, told them what I was thinking, and was promptly fired. It took less than five minutes.

Um, excuse me? Did I misread the answers to my prayers? I never actually heard the words, "You're fired," but in an instant it was clear, and what I had spent months avoiding and the entire afternoon the day before praying about, was over.

After a ten-minute passionate rant at the boss that I am not proud of, I said a few goodbyes, grabbed a couple belongings, and walked out. I got in my car, closed the door, took a deep breath, and a calm started washing over me. *Well, I guess it was time,* I thought to myself. In all the prayers I had prayed in the previous months, one thing I was certain of was that God would get me out of that situation when I needed to be out. Apparently, that was it.

When I got home, reality started setting in. We were again without an income. Health insurance would go away. This would become our biggest challenge yet. It would test the foundation of everything we believed and what we built our marriage on. Could we stay true to ourselves and committed to each other through another storm?

My wife was artfully calm. She did not freak out or have much to say. I told her I wanted to go for a walk and collect my thoughts, so she took the kids to the neighborhood pool for a morning swim.

I found out later that she broke down at the pool. Once again faced with an uncertain future, she was hit with fear. I don't blame her. I'm surprised she didn't show those emotions right when I walked in the door. In hindsight, had she initially reacted emotionally, negatively, or fearfully, it might have set the tone for the months to come. It certainly would have been much more difficult to fully experience what came next.

I took a prayer walk around our neighborhood. Nature has a way of helping me feel closer to God, and I had some questions to ask him. Big questions. I thought about how much we had in our savings account, the value we had lost on our house since we bought it (we were in the midst of the 2007-2008 real estate crash) and the fact that at some point we would be forced to either make early withdrawals from our meager retirement accounts or ask my in-laws if we could shack up with them until we could afford to support ourselves and their two grandchildren. That point was coming fast. We only had a few short months.

Quickly into that saunter, another peace came over me, as if I was being shown exactly how to construct a puzzle from scattered parts. First, I knew we had enough money to last longer than two months. Not much longer, but I knew it was at least that. So I gave myself permission not to worry about anything until after Halloween, which was two months away. After having been previously out of work for fifteen months, I gave myself two to live in peace, relying on nothing but faith. It made no sense. Why was I not anxious? Why did everything feel right again?

I once heard former NFL quarterback-turned-announcer Joe Theismann discussing the difficulties of gaining respect as a young quarterback in the league. He said, "Early in your career, if you're lucky enough to be in a situation late in a close game where it is fourth down and twenty, and you convert a first down ... your teammates will follow you anywhere." If you're lucky enough? Well, we were lucky. It was fourth and twenty in our game of life, and I knew just who to hand the ball off to.

I started to see this situation as an opportunity. Not an opportunity for me, but a chance for us to rely so much on God that He could show his power, protection, and authority over our family. I could have easily looked at this as a gigantic failure on my part. I was in my late thirties and broke, with no job or job prospects, and a family that relied on me to provide. If you had asked me twenty years earlier, I expected to be a millionaire by this time—but none of that mattered. What mattered was how we were going to manage going forward, and the best future for us was in God's hands, not mine. I surrendered my pride and ego, knowing that He can take care of my wife and kids much better than I can.

Perfectly set up to put all our reliance on the Creator of heaven and earth, I resolved not to worry about a thing until Halloween. After that, I told myself and God, I would flip out with worry as much as I wanted!

The next piece of the puzzle was how to conduct a job search, and I saw a vision for how to go about it that was different than anything I had tried before. Somehow, I knew it would work. I also felt the urge to take a week to finish a screenplay I had been toiling over for months. Crazy? Perhaps. But that screenplay taught me lessons about love and marriage that I wouldn't have gained had I not completed it. And my wife was fully supportive. She understood the plan and had peace as well. We were in lock step, walking forward on a foundation of faith and trust.

By mid-October, I still did not have a job. The peace-of-mind clock was ticking, but I had a couple interviews lined up. One was a phone interview with the largest company in its industry. That call with the hiring manager was disastrous. I botched every answer. I fumbled the most basic questions, such as "How did you hear about the job?" and "What interests you about it?" When we got to the end, I was expecting to hear him politely say, "Thanks for your time, but don't call us, we'll call you." Instead, he said, "Well, we'd like you to come in for a face-to-face interview with some other folks." *Excuse me? Were you listening to my babble for the last twenty minutes?*

A week later, I had met with two vice presidents and was

offered the job. The salary was exactly what I had been making at the previous company. Oh, and the day I accepted their offer ... was the day before Halloween. In the most severe housing crisis and downward-spiraling economy of my lifetime, I was fired by the worst company I've ever worked for, then subsequently hired by the best company I've had the privilege of working for. All in less than two months. These are just the highlights of that two-month period. There were many more unexplainable things that happened, reinforcing our belief in God's guidance over us.

In this moment, we did not waver from our priorities, and we persevered through the challenges. Our faith was greater than our fear. We put our family first in all our decisions. Our marriage is the nucleus of our family, and having recently recommitted our vow to each other—in good times and bad—our support for each other never diminished. Above our marriage, God is most important and, most importantly, in control. He is the source and guide for our marriage, a marriage that strengthens our family and lifts our faith. This is a continual cycle that has sustained us through every success and failure.

Looking back at the vision I received after getting fired, I have no explanation for how things worked out the way they did apart from Divine guidance. Nothing made sense. The peace, patience, diligence, and expediency with which I both finished the screenplay and found a new job was so out of the ordinary it had to be God's hand leading it.

Sometimes, the moments we see as challenges or tragedies in our life or marriage could be opportunities for us to lean more heavily on God and, in turn, realize that leaning on him is precisely what we need to be doing all the time. My wife and I don't just look to each other to solve all our problems. That type of reliance can lead to resentment and blame between each other, particularly if things don't turn out how you think they should. Instead, we turn toward each other and, together, look up for answers. Then we do our part to assist.

By the end of that year, the company that had fired me was closing its doors and getting sued by the banks it had defrauded. It was another reminder that the day they kicked me out, "it was time" for God to get me out of there. I was spared from having to go through any of that mess.

"What an opportunity for God to show his power, protection, and authority over our family!" That was the initial thought that had given me peace after losing my job, and God did not disappoint.

Come together. Look up for guidance. Then do your part and do not give up. Overcoming the struggle can become the super glue that binds you together, stronger, forever.

PERSONAL REFLECTION

OBJECTIVE

To determine what priority you give marriage and make sure your actions are supporting it appropriately.

SECTION I: WHERE IS "FAMILY" IN ORDER OF PRIORITY IN YOUR LIFE?

Think about the major parts of your life. Rank them in order of how you prioritize them, such as: Faith, Family, Friends, Career, Leisure, Volunteering, etc.

_____

_____

_____

Are your schedule, activities, and actions congruent with those priorities? If not, what would need to change for them to be more congruent?

_____

_____

_____

SECTION II: WHAT IS YOUR DATING LIFE LIKE?

What is the purpose of dating someone when you are single?

_____

_____

_____

How often do you and your spouse date? Do you have enough quality time together?

_____

_____

_____

What can you do to ensure that you have the time you need together to keep your relationship nourished?

_____

_____

_____

SECTION III: WHETHER YOU ARE MARRIED OR SINGLE, WHAT TYPE OF SPOUSE DO YOU WANT TO BE?

What qualities or characteristics do you want to have?

_____

_____

_____

What do you want your marriage to be like?

_____

_____

_____

SECTION IV: WHAT IS A MAJOR CHALLENGE YOU ARE GOING THROUGH RIGHT NOW IN YOUR MARRIAGE OR RELATIONSHIP?

Does it feel like you are going through this alone?

_____

_____

_____

How can you and your spouse commit to each other, to get through this challenge together and strengthen your marriage in the process?

_____

_____

_____

ACTIVITIES

For the next four weeks, have one "Communication" date per week. Set a time specifically to catch up and discuss with each other anything you've been going through or that is on your mind.

Within the next three months, plan a "Surprise" date with your spouse. Make it special for him/her! Think outside of the box.

Create something romantic or what you know your spouse would enjoy and appreciate.

Pray together once a day for an entire week.

CHALLENGE

Schedule a renewal of your vows on your next anniversary. It could be a large celebration or simple and small. Just do it!

HUMILITY

TRADING PLACES

"Your grandfather once told me it was okay to think about what you want to do until it was time to start doing what you were meant to do."

- The Rookie

What do you really want from your marriage? Ultimately, our actions are a means to an end, to something we want, right? All the effort we put into it is futile unless it bears fruit. We could continue to traverse valleys together and overcome anything life puts in our way, but if we aren't growing closer and experiencing deeper love along the way, what is the point? Prioritizing your marriage, giving all of yourself to your spouse, and vice versa, feeding the relationship, and putting God above it ... does it pay off? Where does it lead us? Is it all worth it?

Yes, a million times over.

Our primary objective has been: Take care of each other. Everything else is secondary. For us, this has provided simplicity and clarity in an ever-changing, confusing, and complicated world. Don't get me wrong, we have busy lives just like everyone, with many responsibilities and obligations to other people and the world. However, to simplify the mess that is life, our focus is always: You take care of me, I'll take care of you, and then we'll help change the world around us together. In doing that, we have experienced blessings we might not have otherwise.

This sense of clarity was never more evident than during a conversation I had with my father-in-law at our kitchen table several years ago. Like many married men, the relationship I have with my father-in-law can be fickle. We have some commonalities and some opposing views. We have butted heads a few times, but he has always been accepting of me and supportive of my dreams.

Perhaps the biggest thing we share is a love and value of family. "Is there anything better than watching kids run up a hill?" he asked once, with a grin on his face while watching his four young grandchildren try to race a young yellow Labrador Retriever up a steep slope in my brother-in-law's backyard. He stood watching with a blissful twinkle in his eye that grandparents get when filled with unconditional love.

The dinner table conversation he and I had was centered on family—which included my wife, his daughter. After everyone else had made their way to bed, we discussed the journey of life and my current place in it. A few changes were converging, causing me to consider what I was focusing on and how I was using my time. I'd had a nearly fifteen-year "relationship" with writing that had become stagnant. It felt like, maybe, we needed a break from each other. I had been pushing at it for so long and wondered if I had forgotten the purpose for which I had started doing it in the first place. At the same time, I was progressing at my job and the company was expanding. Similarly, my wife was starting to get back into the classroom as a teacher's assistant, a position that would be a step to running her own class again. Our kids were getting older, and the remaining years of influence we had on them were dwindling. All of this led me to a crossroads.

Personal goals should be reviewed and evaluated periodically to confirm if we are still on the right path, heading in the direction we want to go. We should do the same for our marriages, taking stock of how strong they are and where they are heading. We should see our marriages for what they are, confirm if they are what we want them to be, and make any changes to set a better course or to avoid pitfalls.

I'd spent the previous four years working on a screenplay that ended up going nowhere. Add that to several other years of writing on my own, chasing a dream that cost nights, weekends, and some holidays away from my family, and I was concerned it would start taking a toll on our marriage. It all added up to years of sacrifice on my wife's part, sacrifice for my benefit, without as much of my own sacrifice for her sake. Was it time to give up the dream altogether or at least take a break from the endless pursuit?

This is a tricky dilemma, and I don't think there is a common solution for every individual or marriage. There are essentially three choices: We can go after a dream at all costs, give up on the dream entirely, or try to achieve the dream while maintaining other parts of our lives that are also valuable to us. To achieve a dream, we must take risks. The question is, how much are we willing to risk?

Sylvester Stallone has been an inspiration to me ever since I was a kid, first through his movies, then as a person when I learned of his own real-life story in the creation and making of *Rocky*. Stallone had a dream of being an actor, and he eliminated all other options and pursued that as his only path. Unable to find consistent work as an actor, he eventually lost the heat in his apartment, sold his dog, and hocked his wife's jewelry, simply trying to pay the bills and survive. He believed that if he gave in and got a regular job to help pay the bills, he would get seduced by comfort and lose some of the relentless drive he had for acting, that drive being his biggest and perhaps only advantage in that pursuit. We all know the story after that—he created one of film's most iconic characters that has entertained and inspired audiences for almost half a century and was one of the movie industry's biggest box office draws of the 1980s. He got his dream and then some, but it cost him his marriage at the time. Was it worth it? Depends on how you look at it and what the most important objective is.

On the flip side, most people either give up on their dreams, or never go after them in the first place, from fear of losing what they have. This is the easiest path to take. You can't fail if you never try. No risk, no pain … but no reward.

Perhaps the most difficult path is to try achieving both a personal dream and a strong marriage concurrently. This requires a greater commitment to prioritization, sacrifice, and selflessness. This was the path I had taken. When I started writing, one of the first pieces of advice I got was to move to Los Angeles, because it would allow me to network and open doors that are much more difficult to open elsewhere. I didn't want to do that to my family. We preferred living in the southeast and closer to our parents and siblings. So we stayed put, making the dream a little more distant, but still highly attainable. I didn't want to achieve the dream if it meant replacing my marriage or family. I wanted both, and that's how I've lived my life. It's what I have always believed is best for us.

Along with a personal dream, I have also had an aspirational vision for a close, dynamic, loving family. My wife and I share this vision. The personal goals—those were just mine. While my wife fully supported them, they weren't hers. She understood what I wanted to achieve and why, but she didn't really care if I made movies or became rich. She sacrificed much of her own time solely so I could chase my own desire. A part of me felt awfully selfish about that, and I was getting concerned that my priorities were, or were about to be, out of balance. I didn't want to risk tipping the scales and becoming too much of a *receiver* of love in our marriage without *giving* as much or more back. I needed to figure out how to balance that out.

Mind you, my wife never said anything about our marriage being out of balance, but I saw it. Along with the opportunities being brought before me at work and my wife's impending transition back to the classroom full time, a shift in priority was warranted. The dream was still a dream, but as I told my father-in-law at the kitchen table that night, "Right now, I need to focus on taking care of my family." Not that I was giving up on the dream; I just made sure priorities were in order. God, marriage, family. Everything else came after those. A part of me started to question if I even had the desire to keep writing. However, there was no question about the desire I had for my wife and family.

That decision marked a definitive shift in our marriage and family dynamic. I no longer stayed up late working on writing projects or tried to get away on weekends to complete additional pages. Family trips became time with our whole family, rather than just my wife and kids while I stayed home to keep working. Removing writing from the top priority for all my free time, I was able to be immersed in my job, getting a managerial role rather quickly. As a screenwriter, I wanted to impact audiences through the stories I told. As a manager, I was able to directly and immediately impact people, both personally and professionally. It was ultimately the same objective in a different, more intimate setting. Achieving goals and in what capacity comes down to perspective.

My wife was on her way to reestablishing her career. While spending three years as a teacher's assistant, she gradually reacquired the credentials necessary to lead a classroom and reignited the passion that earned her the New Teacher of the Year award her first year out of graduate school. Seventeen years after leaving that first job in Atlanta, she once again became a full-time educator of middle-school English and Language Arts.

The decision for her to return to full-time work was not an individual one; it was a collective agreement by our family of four because it would impact all of us. Not that we would have tried to talk my wife out of it if we didn't agree, but *because* she wanted to do it, we all needed to be on board and accept whatever changes would come of it. We knew that pulling this off—both of us working full-time for the first time since we had children—meant adapting some of our habits and expectations. Logistically, who was going to cook dinner every night? Who was going to drive the kids to their activities? Who was going to volunteer in church ministries? Most importantly, how could I support her in what was a demanding job with the same love and intensity with which she had supported me and my writing aspirations? What could I do to help her grow, succeed, and follow her innate passion as a schoolteacher?

We quickly realized that on most days, she was going to be working deep into the evenings. So after years of cooking meals mostly on weekends, I became the regular nightly chef. When you have your priorities in line and act accordingly, regardless of how difficult it might be, it is interesting to see the benefits and blessings that spring up. Shifting food responsibilities was an example. As far as eating habits go, I had a renewed desire to eat as healthy as possible. My daughter, in her youthful and truthful observance, shared with me one night at bedtime, "Daddy, you have a big belly." That's all it took to motivate me to shed the extra pounds I hadn't realized had attached themselves to my waist.

More importantly, we had a minor health scare. My wife had a spot on one of her breasts. It turned out benign, but it highlighted the need to take care of our health. The added stress of being a full-time teacher in today's educational system further emphasized the importance of taking care of her physical and emotional well-being. Removing most of that burden from her shoulders, I now make almost all the breakfasts and lunches and majority of dinners.

In addition to changing our food prep process, we traded some other household roles. Since I was making most of the meals, it made sense that I would also do the grocery shopping. It was a disaster at first. I think the local grocery store changes the location of a few items every week just to mess with me. Thankfully, when our daughter was eight years old, she started baking on her own. Shortly after that, she became my grocery-shopping partner. This was a double blessing. First, she knew exactly where those two or three items were located that I could never find. Second, we had a blast together, and still do. We joke and laugh our way through the store. She thinks it's just grocery shopping, but the experience we have together is much more meaningful.

Overall, I have had more quality time with my kids, more so than I did when I was the only one working. I coached my son's Little League baseball teams. I began volunteering more at church, leading a weekly small group study for middle and high school boys, going on mission trips, and teaching Sunday school classes, all of which either my son or daughter were involved in. For a year, I stayed at home in the morning until my daughter got on the school bus. It was a year of heated Yahtzee contests almost every morning. I also volunteered for some of her dance performances. My relationship with both of my children became richer beyond anything I had imagined.

My relationship with my wife became richer as well. She was growing and engaging in passions she hadn't stoked in years. I was seeing a side of her that I had fallen in love with when we first met. She has fire, pizzazz, and boundless energy when she is engaged in her work. It has been amazing and inspiring to watch. We relate to each other on a deeper level and have become closer.

As far as writing goes, taking some time away from the grind opened my eyes to some stark realizations. When I began my writing journey, it was out of a desire to inspire and encourage people through the platform of a cinematic story. As years went by and we endured long stretches of fiscal famine, writing became one of the options to solve our financial issues. It took my focus off the purpose in my heart and made writing about money. I also realized that I didn't just care about writing and selling screenplays as much as I simply had a passion for finding stories that need to be told, however that may be. "There are so many stories that people should hear, but never will," a friend once said to me, referring to a real-life heroic incident that he witnessed when he was in the military. Whether I write those stories or not, the deepest desire of my soul is simply to find them and help them get told. The break from writing gave me exactly what I needed.

My wife and I began moving together in greater harmony. Supporting and helping her transition back to work, advancing my career through my job, and repurposing my writing efforts have helped us realize collective dreams and goals that had taken a backseat. We have been able to travel more as a family and give more to others, our church, and charities. We have learned to be more generous and focused with our time and resources. In the end, these things are more important to me than simply selling a screenplay and making a movie. Before our family dynamic reshuffling, I had forgotten that.

This experience taught me how important it is to keep assessing your marriage and to be as flexible as you need to be to make your marriage how you want it. Remember, marriage isn't about you, it's about *us*. It is a partnership with a common goal, working together through the obstacles and challenges of life toward that united objective. It doesn't matter who does what or when. Be willing to adapt for the betterment of your marriage and family. That doesn't mean becoming a lapdog and giving up on your dreams. It means maintaining priorities and changing your own if you need to.

You might be saying, "That sounds good in an idealistic world, but my spouse and I are different people with different goals and dreams." True. However, a running back has different objectives than an offensive lineman. The running back's primary purpose is to take the ball and run, so he wants to be nimble and fast, able to avoid as many would-be tacklers as possible. An offensive lineman's primary role is not to avoid tacklers but to intentionally get in their way, in support of the running back trying to work his way around them. He wants to be big, strong, and immovable. That is what those two players get paid to do—the running back runs and the offensive lineman blocks. Sometimes, though, the running back is asked to block as well, so that a different play can be run. Other times, the running back is asked to catch a pass and, on rare occasions, the offensive lineman is asked to catch one as well. While those players have different primary roles, they also take on other roles whenever needed for one common purpose— to move down the field and score a touchdown. In a marriage, we have common goals as well. Sometimes, when the situation or circumstance dictates, we need to be willing to alter or change those individual roles in support of the greater good.

As a team, we should plan and organize to best accomplish our common goals in all seasons of life. We need to guard ourselves against falling into ruts, becoming so locked into playing certain roles that we fail to adjust to the circumstances of the season we are in or are about to head into. The vision we have for our marriage, what we truly want from it, should not diminish because of a change in season. Whether in prosperity or lack, triumph or tragedy, the goals we have for our marriage itself should not be affected.

One of the greatest benefits of "trading places" in the way that my wife and I did was a greater appreciation for each other and the different roles we have taken throughout our relationship. Some couples can do it all—build businesses, have a loving marriage, raise fantastic kids, and realize all their wildest individual dreams—all at the same time. Some. Probably few. Doing it all is not something my wife and I have figured out yet. Until or unless we do, we make sure our marriage and family are the top priorities. I would argue that many couples *think* they can do it all, until they realize they can't. By then, it might be too late.

Individual dreams come and go. What I have learned is that,

whether my personal dreams are succeeding or failing, a loving, thriving marriage leads to hidden blessings and can be the greatest dream of all.

LIKE FATHER-IN-LAW, LIKE SON-IN-LAW

"I will be watching you, studying your every move, and if I find that you are trying to corrupt my firstborn child, I will bring you down, baby. I will bring you down to Chinatown."

- Meet the Parents

When my wife was pregnant with our daughter, I remember standing in the doctor's office talking with the nurse who held the results of our sonagram in her hand.

"Do you want to know if it's a boy or a girl?" she asked.

"No," we both replied.

We wanted it to be a surprise. Staring down at the folder in the nurse's hand, we were two feet away from knowing whether our second child would be a boy or a girl. Secretly, I was hoping for a girl since we already had a boy. I wanted the full experience as a parent and, honestly, wondered if I could love another son as much as I loved my first. It's a strange dilemma that is hard to admit.

Fourteen years after captivating my heart and rocking my

world the moment she was born, my daughter was a freshman in high school and my world was about to get rocked all over again. Whether or not you have a daughter, if you are married or hope to get married someday, what I learned from the moment I am about to share still pertains to you.

It started when I was standing in the side yard of a friend's house, holding a plate full of crawfish. It was an annual boil with good friends and acquaintances. I was having difficulty enjoying myself, awaiting the arrival of someone who was not a guest at the party.

A few days earlier, my daughter was talking with one of her friends at school about a farm-to-table restaurant in our hometown that she hadn't been to but she thought sounded interesting. "We have to go!" announced a boy also in the conversation, and a plan was hatched. My daughter's friend had a boyfriend. The couple, my daughter, and this *other* boy planned a dinner date that wasn't an actual date. Sound familiar? I was told the boy's grandfather would be driving them there and eating with them. So I signed off on it. Begrudgingly.

Waiting for them to arrive at the party to pick up my daughter, I was anxious to see what this other boy was like. When the car pulled up, my heart started beating faster. My palms got sweaty. Before I knew it, my daughter had hopped into the backseat with her girlfriend.

I slowly walked over to the car to make sure everything was on the up and up—and quickly found out that it wasn't. The grandfather climbed out of the driver's seat and met me at the trunk. After a customary handshake and awkward smile, he said, "Well, my grandson just told me that they only have a table for four because the restaurant didn't have any with five seats." Which meant the grandfather would *not* be eating with them after all.

"Really," I scoffed.

"That's what he said." The grandfather shrugged. I could see the back of the boy's head through the rear window. The grandfather knew the kid was lying. I knew he was lying. "I figure I'll just drop them off at the restaurant, drive around for an hour, then go back and pick them up. But whatever you want to do is fine with me," the old man said. "I'll understand."

Whatever I want to do? Did he mean that? Because what I wanted to do was yank his grandson out of the front seat by the collar, pin him up against the door, and scare the scheming lies right out of him!

While that might have been the most satisfying action to take, I realized there were other options. I could tell my daughter to get out of the car and not allow her to go, or I could do nothing and let her go anyway. None appeared to be ideal options—except scaring the kid half to death. My parental instincts were telling me not to let her go, to take a stand now, or this kind of situation would keep happening and only get worse. I fast forwarded the next few years in my mind and saw my daughter at fifteen, sixteen, or eighteen years old and the boys who would be conspiring against me so they could get to her. It was more cringe-worthy than any horror film I've ever watched.

I decided to do nothing … right then. I thought of the embarrassment it would have caused my daughter if I told her to get out of the car and forbid her to go, and what it might do to our relationship as she was just starting the difficult years of high school. I weighed the immediate consequences and, realizing she wasn't compromised or in any danger, I resolved to show her some trust. After all, she was going to have dinner with a stupid boy who thought she was cool.

Not a big deal. They were fourteen and being driven around by a gullible grandpa. The dinner was more like a play date than a romantic date. At least, that's what I convinced myself to keep my sanity that evening.

A couple hours later, grandpa returned with the kiddos and I was right, it had been a harmless excursion. At home that night, my wife and I had "the talk" with our daughter. We told her how the boy tricked his grandfather and, while relatively innocent, it was still a concern. If he was willing to lie about something as benign as an early evening dinner, what else might he be willing to lie about? The worst part was that he lied to *her* about it. She honestly believed the grandfather was going to be with them at the restaurant. You might be thinking I am a naïve father, but there are times when you know your kids are telling the truth and when they aren't. This was one of those times when my wife and I both knew she was being honest with us.

"There was only one person in the car this afternoon that I trusted—you," I told her. That included the grandfather. We wanted her to know that regardless of what anyone else does, we expect her to make good decisions and we trust her to do so because she has earned it. We also told her that this boy, as Robert DeNiro put it in *Meet the Parents,* was outside the Bellini family circle of trust and would not be allowed in, at least for a very long time. I know what teenage boys are like. I was one. I thought the things they think. I wanted the things they want. I am cursed with the knowledge of understanding what is rattling between the ears of every immature boy who's ever roamed the halls of high school.

All of this got me thinking—thinking of renting a cabin in

the woods and living there by myself until my daughter's teenage years are over! The fear of what these years are going to bring is real. Unfortunately, as much as I would love to, we can't just skip past them. In my life to this point, I have been the boy and the young man in pursuit of the girl. I have been the boyfriend and the husband. For the first time, I was a father who has a daughter, and I started thinking like one. Other boys would be in pursuit of her and, before I know it, there will be a boyfriend and perhaps a husband.

A husband to my daughter. The idea frightens me. Why? Because no boy or man will ever … ever … *ever* live up to the expectation I want for my daughter. I have an unattainable standard of perfection that no man can achieve. It is an unrealistic hope I think most of us have for our children, whether we realize it or not. My love for my children is unconditional. There is nothing I wouldn't do for them. I would willingly give my life if it were necessary to save theirs.

How could there be a man in the entire world who would come to love my daughter in the same way? It seems impossible.

As I pondered all these fears after my daughter's dinner with Lying Larry, my thoughts turned to another daughter in our family—my wife. She is a daughter as well, with a father who thinks the same way about her that I think about mine. I'm sure he has the same unconditional love, same willingness to trade his life for hers, and same unrealistic expectations for me, the man who asked for his daughter's hand in marriage.

I realize there are bad fathers and bad parents in life. There are some who aren't necessarily as loving or giving, and some who are even abusive. I am not talking about those parents. I can only speak to my own experience, in my own family. After twenty-five years, I know my father-in-law's heart. I know his love for his children, and I know my love for mine. The love we both have is unmistakably and unwaveringly absolute.

Seeing your wife as someone else's daughter rather than just your spouse offers a different, thought-provoking perspective. That "someone else" hopes you are every bit of the husband that you want another man to be for your own daughter. This perspective prompted me to measure myself as a husband by the expectations I have for the kind of man I want for my daughter. Am I being for my wife what I want another man to be for her?

This was an eye-opening, candid self-reflection. It has allowed me to see things I need to improve on and ways I can treat my wife better. It has also renewed a sense of commitment and dedication to her and to our marriage. I consider myself an above-average husband. I am resolutely devoted and dedicated to my wife and marriage. However, looking at her in this light has raised the standard of the type of husband I want to be. I have an even greater level of appreciation for and dedication to my wife.

I wonder if my wife had a similar experience when my mother passed away a few years ago. I was the apple of my mother's eye. Moving a thousand miles from home only intensified that. Our wedding photos are quite telling about what my mother was feeling the day my wife and I got married. In every one of the professional pictures, my mother looks miserably sad. My wife and I have had a good laugh while flipping through these pictures and seeing how devastated and depressed she looked. We can laugh about it because the night before the wedding, my mom was her typical bundle of joyous energy, and after the wedding, she was dancing the night away at the reception. However, in the hours leading up to the ceremony at the church, she must have been focusing on something else. Did she feel like she was losing a son? Being replaced?

During the last few years of my mother's life, we grew even closer as she spent them battling cancer. Though we didn't see each other more than a couple times a year, we talked almost every day. When she finally succumbed to the disease, I'd bet my wife also had a renewed sense of purpose in our marriage—a responsibility to live up to the expectations that the woman in our wedding photos, who appeared so heartbroken, had for her son. I have never discussed this with my wife, but it may have been a symbolic and ultimate passing of the torch from the first woman in my life to the last.

Men, find reasons to keep raising the standard for the husband you are and whom your wife needs. Women, do the same. Our spouses aren't just our spouses. They are also sons and daughters, brothers and sisters, and fathers and mothers. They are a lot of things to a lot of people. We have a greater responsibility to love and serve them than anyone else. We have more to do than just live with them and get along. We are called to love and love more deeply, more intimately, than anyone else. It is the greatest responsibility of our lives.

THE WRITING ON THE WALL

"Some days your mother and me loved each other. Other days we had to work at it. You never see the hard days in a photo album. But those are the ones that get you from one happy snapshot to the next."

- Just Married

Initially, this chapter was going to be a short epilogue with some closing thoughts. While writing it, however, I realized that I was living in the next major moment of my marriage. Reflecting on the moments that have made the biggest impact on our marriage has been healing, inspiring, and rejuvenating. It has reminded me how good marriage can be, how difficult it is, and how to persevere amid the ups and down. Throughout the writing of this book, I have laughed and cried, felt chills and been filled with gratitude. It has reminded me of the husband I want to be and how to be him.

Our marriage is far from perfect. Perhaps by the world's standards it looks great, but by our standards and God's standards, we have work to do. Just like every other married couple—we have bad habits, destructive tendencies, and selfish desires. We get upset, short, and sarcastic with each other. We are continually trying to figure out how to work hard, play hard, and maintain our closeness and peace of mind. The moments in this book do not tell our whole story, but they have taught us valuable lessons, and have been the building blocks for a marriage that has thrived for over two decades, despite our shortcomings.

As I said in the beginning, we are not unique. What makes us special is the same thing that makes you special—the truth that every one of us has a story to tell. We are all living through this adventure of life, creating a lasting story through the decisions we make and the actions we take.

What story are you writing in your marriage, or planning to write in a marriage someday? Is it worth telling? Is it worth living? What are the major moments that have influenced your marriage—positively and negatively? Assess how you worked through them and how they have impacted your actions, words, and beliefs.

If you are not married yet, be cognizant of the fact that these moments will occur and decide what kind of spouse you want to be when they show up.

Building, maintaining, and growing a successful marriage is no different than how we would approach any other goal or aspiration in life. Have an ultimate vision for what you want, be honest about where your marriage is right now, and figure out what you need to do to make it what you want it to be.

Since the introductory chapter, you may have noticed there are not many references to ultra running throughout the book. That's because we should not hyper focus on the overwhelming concept of a lifelong commitment. Remember to stay committed to the moment. Like the day I attempted to give everything I could possibly give to my wife, through an early morning wake up, to a stressful business trip, and a late-night grocery list review. That is how we take our marriage the distance, and make the distance worth taking … one day, one step, one moment at a time.

Both ultra running and marriage take:

1. Preparation (Finding Me). Building a solid foundation that will set us up for a stronger race, and a healthier marriage. Discovering our strengths and weaknesses will help us build ourselves for a better result.

2. Teamwork (Becoming We). Though running is a solo sport, there comes a point in any ultra race when everyone needs help. Whether it is food, water, first aid, or encouragement to keep going, everyone needs a team. No one will finish otherwise. In marriage, we are two individuals who form one team. We can't complete the journey alone.

3. Focus (Priority). Keeping our minds on the moment at hand, rather than the entirety of the race to come, is critical to believing we can continue moving forward, and even getting stronger as we go. When running, it's just us and the trail ahead. Nothing else matters. In marriage, nothing should matter as much as that relationship.

4. Surrender (Humility). At some point in a long race, pain will get intense. We may even wonder if enduring it will eventually pay off the way we hope. We must be willing to surrender the comfort we so desire and peace we desperately crave and find a way to do whatever we can to reach the ultimate destination. In marriage, we must humble ourselves to do whatever it takes to love, and keep loving, to get to

the other side where our grandest dreams reside.

A loving, thriving, happy marriage all comes down to the choices we make. Several years ago, I was having a phone conversation with my father about someone who was contemplating walking away from marriage. My dad was assisting with the exit strategy. I knew from firsthand experience that the spouse being left behind could be a selfish, childish jerk. However, being an advocate of marriage, I asked a few questions. Without any knowledge of abuse or infidelity, I wondered what led to the decision to leave? Had they been to counseling? Had they tried everything they could to make the marriage work, or was running away from the problems just the path of least resistance? Did they even know what the primary problems were?

The tension was building in our dialogue. It may have seemed that I was not being supportive or understanding, or that I was admonishing my father for helping, but I was simply sticking up for the most important and impactful part of our lives other than our relationship with God. I was sticking up for marriage. My father didn't see it that way, and he lashed out.

"That's easy for you to say!" he yelled from the phone. "You're down there (in Tennessee), all happy!"

At that, I nearly lost my own temper. *Easy? EASY?* the voice inside my head screamed again and again.

Please do not think that someone else's marriage is easy just because they are happy or appear happier than you. Marriage is not easy. For anyone. It wasn't easy to support my then girlfriend going to lunch with her old flame to see if their spark would reignite. Nothing about having and raising children is easy—from postpartum depression, to disagreements about parenting rules and styles, to complete loss of intimacy at times. Being financially broke, with two kids under the age of five, when neither my wife nor I was working, and being unsure how we were going to pay our mortgage—was not easy. Mistakes, bad decisions, hurtful words ... they touch every marriage, and none of it is easy to repair and restore. Happiness is not easy. It is a choice.

Most importantly, it takes two people to make that choice and to make a marriage work. One person cannot do the work for both and uphold a marriage on their own. The point of a marriage is to make a pledge, a promise, to live as one, act as a team, and make choices for the betterment of that team. It is not about benefiting one over the other.

Professional athletes, musicians, painters, those with tremendous skills or a successful business, make what they do look easy. We only see the end results—the plays, the songs, the works of art. What we don't see are the countless hours of hard work they put into their craft and all the times they got up early when everyone else was sleeping and stayed up late after everyone else went to bed. We don't see the times they said "No" to the things that would keep them from becoming who they wanted to become. The moments described in this book took effort. Living through the fluctuations of life in between these moments took effort. To maintain what we have and to grow it even further is going to take more effort.

When most of these moments occurred, I did not recognize them as being significant at the time, and I did not see how they would define the marriage that my wife and I have today. The advice from my grandfather about the secret of life was one of those moments. Others were obvious difference makers, turning points, and building blocks—such as the time I got angry at my wife right before her dance audition. I knew our actions and the outcomes of those certain moments would have lifelong effects on our relationship.

Think again. What are those moments that have defined your own marriage or relationship? What is it about those times that have had a lasting impact? What are the choices and actions that led to your current state? What is it about the positive experiences that have strengthened your marriage? What did you focus on and what actions did you take? What about the negative experiences can you learn from and do better next time? It is important to take stock of where we are and identify what got us here.

Over time, we tend to diminish the strength of our foundation, forgetting how difficult things were and what it took to get through them. We forget the effort involved. We assume that, because we already put in the effort, we should get through challenges and obstacles more easily or, worse, that we shouldn't have to go through them at all. However, a mile is still a mile, no matter how many of them we run. The distance doesn't get shorter based on our past experiences. As couples, we must continue to keep stepping up to the challenges and major moments in our relationships in order to maintain what we have and grow toward what we desire. These moments will keep coming. More are on the way, and I thank God for them! I thank God this book is not the end but just a snapshot in time of this journey we are taking together. We must remember the effort it took to get through the moments that are behind us, that defined how we got to where we are today, if we are to reap the rewards of the moments that are before us.

For my wife and me, the formula has been simple, though not easy. Before we even met, we found ourselves and became comfortable with who we were created to be. Together, we became a team, and we live knowing that we are stronger and better as two than we can ever be as one. We set our priorities together and stick to them, with a firm foundation and reliance on God as our guide and source of strength and well-being. We feed and fuel our marriage and continually strive to make it better. Everything we ever want is with each other.

Ultimately, the question is this: What do you want your marriage to be? I argue that it should be the top priority, but it is up to you to decide what you want and believe. My hope is that you choose each other, that you choose love, commitment, and perseverance. If more husbands and wives not only stay connected in lasting relationships but also do it lovingly, imagine the impact it would have in our world. If more of our children were raised in loving, dedicated families, we would see a change in our culture greater than any time in our history. I am convinced of it.

I recently had a vision. In it, I was walking through a public park. Children were playing in the open field. A dog was chasing a frisbee thrown by its owner. In the distance, I saw my grandfather sitting alone on a bench. I made my way over and sat down next to him. We both stared straight ahead.

"I owe this to you," I said, as I handed him a copy of this book.

He smirked with one cheek, the way he always did. "I always said you were going places," he replied.

Then he flipped through the pages of the book, with a wider grin now on his face. "These are the places I was talking about."

I leave you with a challenge. Whether you are single or are in a relationship and have been together for a day, a year, twenty or fifty years, the challenge is the same. Continue showing up and stepping up to the moments that define you. Keep charging up the mountain to get to the peak, time and time again. As in any other aspect of life, marriage is a continued progression up to peaks and down through valleys. If it weren't, it wouldn't be as exciting a journey. Embrace every bit of it. The valleys can be more comfortable. It takes little effort to stay there, but the view isn't as grand. Climbing toward the peak, on the other hand, is difficult, tiring, and sometimes painful. Climbing takes time, sweat, and often blood; but it is the only way we can get to the top, where we can appreciate, enjoy, and benefit from the most majestic views.

On the way to your own ultra marriage, keep loving, keep going, and keep growing through it together, one step, one moment at a time.

PERSONAL REFLECTION

OBJECTIVE
To continue growing and strengthening your marriage.

SECTION I: DO YOU FEEL TAKEN ADVANTAGE OF IN ANY PART OF YOUR RELATIONSHIP?

Do you believe that you are doing more than you should? Are you doing less?

_____

_____

_____

Are there any ways in which you can help your spouse more?

_____

_____

_____

SECTION II: HOW DO YOU AND YOUR SPOUSE DIVIDE RESPONSIBILITIES?

What is the goal of accomplishing those responsibilities?

_____

_____

_____

Are you working together for a common purpose? If not, what can you do to partner in common objectives?

_____

_____

_____

Are you willing to shift your personal desires for the benefit of the marriage, if necessary?

_____

_____

_____

SECTION III: DO YOU HAVE A VISION OF WHAT YOU WANT YOUR MARRIAGE TO BE LIKE IN THE FUTURE?

What are you doing that is great, that you want to keep doing to move toward a spectacular future together?

_____

_____

_____

What needs to be better?

_____

_____

_____

What have you never done that you want to do together?

_____

_____

_____

SECTION IV: IF YOU ARE SINGLE

What about you would make a great spouse?

_____

_____

_____

What do you need to improve on to become even better prepared?

_____

_____

_____

What do you want to do in your marriage? That is, what do you want to accomplish or experience with your future spouse?

_____

_____

_____

ACTIVITIES

Think about the future. Write out what you want your marriage to be like. Make it an ultimate vision. Then make a plan and schedule actions that will move you toward your ultimate marriage.

CHALLENGE

Trade places for an entire weekend! Whatever you normally do within the context of your marriage and/or family, do the opposite. At the end of the weekend, go on a date and discuss what you learned.

APPENDIX

Following are the verses in which the apostle Paul sets up and describes what a marital relationship should look like. There are one or two aspects of this that we tend to get hung up on, leading us to dismiss the entire instruction as antiquated and out of touch with modern relationships in the world today. I will break down how it speaks to me as to how I view marriage.

From Ephesians 5:

21 Submit to one another out of reverence for Christ.

22 Wives, submit yourselves to your own husbands as you do to the Lord. 23 For the husband is the head of the wife as Christ is the head of the church, his body, of which he is the Savior. 24 Now as the church submits to Christ, so also wives should submit to their husbands in everything.

25 Husbands, love your wives, just as Christ loved the church and gave himself up for her 26 to make her holy, cleansing her by the washing with water through the word, 27 and to present her to himself as a radiant church, without stain or wrinkle or any other blemish, but holy and blameless. 28 In this same way, husbands ought to love their wives as their own bodies. He who loves his wife loves himself. 29 After all, no one ever hated their own body, but they feed and care for their body, just as Christ does the church— ³⁰ *for we are members of his body.* ³¹ *"For this reason a man will leave his father and mother and be united to his wife, and the two will become one flesh."* ³² *This is a profound mystery—but I am talking about Christ and the church.* ³³ *However, each one of you also must love his wife as he loves himself, and the wife must respect her husband.*

It is easy to see what is so controversial about this passage. In it, Paul asserts that "the husband is head of the wife" and that "wives should submit to their husbands in everything." Admittedly, reading just those two verses causes my forehead to wrinkle and question Paul's guidance. It clearly comes across as an instruction to subservience. However, if we first back up one verse, consider it all in context, and even connect it to similar guidance the apostle Peter wrote in his first book, we can see this in its entirety, from a very different light and, I believe, how it was meant to be understood.

²¹ *Submit to one another out of reverence for Christ.*

Verse 21 of this passage is very rarely mentioned. With it, Paul begins this entire section by asking Christians to submit to each other. As he then goes on to talk specifically about wives and husbands, verse 21 presupposes that he is instructing BOTH wives and husbands to submit to each other.

This overarching view gets lost. I am not certain why, unless we simply get so outraged by the words he uses to coach wives that we become blind and deaf to the remaining instruction.

²² *Wives, submit yourselves to your own husbands as you do to the Lord.*

²⁵ Husbands, love your wives, just as Christ loved the church and gave himself up for her

Verses 22 and 25 are two descriptions of the same perspective, that is, to submit to each other. To wives, he repeats the word "submit." To husbands, he introduces it as "love," but then defines it to mean giving yourself up for her. In other words, sacrificing yourself for her good, just as Christ sacrificed himself for the church. To both husbands and wives, he is not saying that marriage is 50-50. He is not saying it is 100-50, that wives should submit fully and husbands should take what they can get. He is telling both that their marriage should be 100-100, full submission to each other.

The apostle Peter sets up his message to wives in a similar way.

From 1 Peter 2:

²¹ To this you were called, because Christ suffered for you, leaving you an example, that you should follow in his steps.

Peter goes on in the next few verses to describe what this example that Jesus provided looks like. That is, refusing to retaliate for insults or make threats when suffering. Then he tells wives the following:

From 1 Peter 3:

...in the same way submit yourselves to your own husbands so that, if any of them do not believe the word, they may be won over without words by the behavior of their wives, ²when they see the purity and reverence of your lives.

Wow! Peter is asking wives to mimic Jesus.

Notice, in a time when women were not highly esteemed (to say the least), Peter speaks to the women first, encouraging them to act Christ-like. He didn't directly tell husbands to be this way, and I expect it is because there was largely a problem with men at that time. I am not an historical scholar, but I imagine that back then, many men did not treat women well. After all, even having made large strides against this attitude, it is still a battle that is being fought today in many ways, two thousand years later.

Take Adam, for example, the initial man. God created him first, before woman, and quickly realized that it was not good for him to be alone. Think about that even in today's environment. Leave a boy (or man) to his own devices, and he might literally destroy himself. Man needed someone else to keep him in line. He needed woman. Husbands need wives in the very same way.

Peter described Jesus as being ridiculed, insulted, and mistreated. Peter is relating a woman's (and a wife's) plight to that of Jesus. He is putting them in the same light as the Lord. Again, think about how radical this was for the time period, when women were treated as less human in some ways. Peter implores wives to set an example for the men in their lives, just as Jesus set an example for all of us.

⁶ *You are her daughters if you do what is right and do not give way to fear.*

He is challenging wives to lead by example and not succumb to fear.

Back to Paul's letter to the Ephesians.

From Ephesians 5:

²³ *For the husband is the head of the wife as Christ is the head of the church, his body, of which he is the Savior.*

Verse 23 is another statement that causes us to cringe, because it suggests that the husband is head of the wife (as if men need more fodder for their ego). Consider again the time when this was written. If a husband was seen as the "head of the wife," it may logically have been because he was just physically stronger.

[28] In this same way, husbands ought to love their wives as their own bodies. He who loves his wife loves himself. [29] After all, no one ever hated their own body, but they feed and care for their body, just as Christ does the church—

In verses 28-29, Paul tells husbands how to love their wives, saying to "feed and care for" them, just as they would their own bodies. He may not have been talking about a specific hierarchical structure between husbands and wives, but rather how they provide for each other's needs. Walmart and Costco did not exist back then. Families took care of themselves. Paul is imploring men to do their part in this construct.

Similarly, in 1 Peter 3, Peter writes:

[7] Husbands, in the same way be considerate as you live with your wives, and treat them with respect as the weaker partner and as heirs with you of the gracious gift of life, so that nothing will hinder your prayers.

Again, in general, men are physically stronger than women. Peter is demanding that husbands not use their overpowering strength to mistreat their wives. He is telling them to be considerate and to "treat them with respect." He would not have written this if it was not a significant problem in their culture. It may have even been standard behavior for husbands to mistreat their wives, without any respect at all. How extreme it must have been for him to tell them directly, "Don't be that way!"

The last part of 1 Peter 3:7 is perhaps the most powerful and telling. He informs husbands that mistreatment of their wives is so egregious that God will not honor their prayers. He may not even listen to them. Peter even says, "So that *nothing* will hinder your prayers." It supposes that the key to having their prayers answered is how they treat their wives. They might sin and make mistakes in other ways and those things may be overlooked in prayer. However, mistreatment of their wives will not be overlooked. How husbands treat wives is a key that either locks or unlocks spiritual power in their lives.

One more log to stoke the fire of opposition to Paul's writing is the repeating of the word "submit":

From Ephesians 5:
24 Now as the church submits to Christ, so also wives should submit to their husbands in everything.

However, we cannot miss the connection to Jesus. Paul says that wives should fully submit, just as the church submits to Christ. It is a petition for complete surrender, not to their detriment or harm, but to the will of Christ, so they and their husbands can reap his rewards of salvation, peace, and love.

In verse 25, Paul gives to husbands the same instruction to love and "give themselves up" for their wives, as Christ did for the church. It is a complete surrender and sacrifice of self, in order for her to become greater, all that she can be:

26 to make her holy, cleansing her by the washing with water through the word, 27 and to present her to himself as a radiant church, without stain or wrinkle or any other blemish, but holy and blameless.

While Paul may use what is deemed as uncomfortable language in today's culture to distinguish the roles of husbands and wives, particularly for that time period, his message is the same for both—to give themselves up in submission to each other. That is, give one hundred percent of themselves in their marriage.

ACKNOWLEDGMENTS

After a failed first attempt at writing a book many years ago, I never imagined that I would try again. Writing a book was as difficult as I anticipated and took a book worth writing for me to start and finish it.

Cindy, my wife, and love of my life, you gave everything on these pages meaning. Thank you for your unconditional love and support, everlasting forgiveness, and giving me a second chance at a first date. You are everything I could ever want and more than I would ever deserve.

To my children, Jonathan and Olivia, you inspire me every day and teach me how to become a better person. I love you more than life itself.

To Grandpa, for encouraging me, loving me for who I am, and helping make me into the man I am today. Thank you for giving me your compass when I was lost. I miss you but know you have been watching over me all these years.

To Grandma, thank you for your prayers, for the strong faith you lived with and for passing that down.

To Jiddo and Grandma Ziter, who showed me what deep, sincere, unconditional love looks like. They set an example of the highest standard as a couple, a standard I will forever try to achieve.

Dad, thank you for recommitting yourself to Mom, and for being a loyal, committed husband for me to watch.

To my mom, for showing me that family is the most important aspect of life. I know you are enjoying Paradise, and I am certain Jesus likes your meatballs as much as I did.

To my in-laws, Rob and Louis Joyner, thank you for supporting Cindy and me in more ways than we can count.

Jim House, my book coach, extended a helping hand when I was perfectly content with simply writing words on a page. Jim, you helped me create a much greater vision for this book and the impact it could have. I cherish that experience and our friendship that came from it.

To Stephanie L. Jones, my publishing coach. I believe we met at just the right time. Your guidance and valuable insight kept my mind at ease and my feet on the ground throughout this awesome process.

To Elaine Starner, my editor. Thank you for providing your expertise, and the kind words and encouragement you offered. You are a such beautiful soul.

I met Tom Prather just before starting the book and had no idea we would build a friendship that led us to work together. You are a special person. Thank you for being a tremendously supportive confidant, and providing your expert creative talent to the cover and branding.

To Jeff Forrester, thank you for replying so enthusiastically to my initial DM! I appreciated your openness in discussing your book, *Unleashed Potential,* and the book writing process. I'm most grateful for your friendship, and for inviting me into the Sons of Thunder, a group of men that inspire me, push me, and help me become a better Christian every day.

To David Berthiaume, for being the first reader of the initial draft (other than my wife) and offering honest constructive feedback. You helped me set the initial tone for this book.

Rob Matthews, Chas Allen, and Jonathan Bellini, thank you so much for offering your eyes, time and invaluable feedback for a final review.

To all my friends, family, and acquaintances that have been supportive along the way. There are too many to count. If you've sent me a message or if we have had a phone call or conversation about the book, every word of encouragement and positive comment has helped lift me up and carry me through this process.

Most importantly, nothing in this book would have been possible without the love and guidance of Almighty God. He created a hole in my life when I was born and started to fill it by knitting my wife just two months later. Before I was even born, You knew I would need a soul mate to make it through this life and You led me to someone with whom I have experienced a slice of heaven on earth. Thank you for whispering in my ear all those times, for guiding Cindy and me throughout our marriage, and for giving us eyes to see, ears to hear, and the heart to understand what You were teaching us and where You were leading us. I can't wait to see where You are taking us next.

NOTES

INTRODUCTION

Hitch. Directed by Andy Tennant, Columbia Pictures, 2005.

MOMENT #1

City Slickers. Directed by Ron Underwood, Castle Rock Entertainment, 1991.

MOMENT #2

Miss Congeniality. Directed by Donald Petrie, Castle Rock Entertainment, 2000.

MOMENT #3

The Vow. Directed by Michael Sucsy, Screen Gems, 2012.

MOMENT #4

Good Will Hunting. Directed by Gus Van Sant, Miramax, 1997.

MOMENT #5

A Walk to Remember. Directed by Adam Shankman, Warner Bros., 2002.

MOMENT #6

Hoosiers. Directed by David Anspaugh, Cinema '84, 1986.

Jerry MaGuire. Directed by Cameron Crowe, TriStar Pictures, 1996.

MOMENT #7

Avengers: Endgame. Directed by Anthony Russo and Joe Russo, Marvel Studios, 2019.

MOMENT #8

Tuesdays with Morrie. Directed by Mick Jackson, Carlton America Harpo Productions, 1999.

MOMENT #9

On Golden Pond. Directed by Mark Rydell, IPC Films, 1981.

MOMENT #10

The Godfather. Directed by Francis Ford Coppola, Paramount Pictures, 1972.

MOMENT #11

Date Night. Directed by Shawn Levy, Twentieth Century Fox, 2010.

MOMENT #12

The Vow. Directed by Michael Sucsy, Screen Gems, 2012.

MOMENT #13

Lost, Season 2, Episode 3. Directed by Jack Bender, Bad Robot, 2005.

MOMENT #14

The Rookie. Directed by John Lee Hancock, Buena Vista Pictures, 2002.

MOMENT #15

Meet the Parents. Directed by Jay Roach, Universal Pictures, 2000.

MOMENT #16

Just Married. Directed by Shawn Levy, Twentieth Century Fox, 2003.

Available on Youtube, Spotify, Apple, and Google Podcasts

Find additional resources online at
www.TheUltraMarriage.com
On Youtube @theultramarriage
On Instagram @ultra_marriage
On Facebook @ultramarriage

Find Mike online at www.mikebellini.com
On Instagram @realmikebellini
On Facebook @mikebellini0708